EXPANDING COOPERATIVE LEARNING
═══ THROUGH ═══
GROUP INVESTIGATION

EXPANDING COOPERATIVE LEARNING
THROUGH
GROUP INVESTIGATION

Yael Sharan   Shlomo Sharan

Teachers College, Columbia University
New York and London

Published by Teachers College Press, 1234 Amsterdam Avenue
New York, New York

Library of Congress Cataloging-in-Publication Data

Sharan, Yael.
   Expanding cooperative learning through group investigation / Yael
Sharan, Shlomo Sharan.
    p.   cm.
   Includes bibliographical references (p.) and index.
   ISBN 0-8077-3191-9 (alk. paper). — ISBN 0-8077-3190-0 (pbk. :
alk. paper)
   1. Group work in education. 2. Cooperativeness. I. Sharan,
Shlomo, 1932- . II. Title.
LB1032.S456 1992
371.3'95—dc20   92-9351

ISBN 0-8077-3191-9
ISBN 0-8077-3190-0 (pbk.)

Printed on acid-free paper

Manufactured in the United States of America

99 98 97 96 95 94 93 92   8 7 6 5 4 3 2 1

To my mother,
Judith Shapiro Gottlieb
and her indomitable spirit
Y.S.

Contents

Preface

Group Investigation is a cooperative learning strategy that integrates interaction and communication in the classroom with the process of academic inquiry. It enables the classroom to become a social system built both on cooperation among students in small groups and on coordination between groups in the classroom. This book provides educators with the background and procedures needed to conduct Group Investigation.

In Group Investigation students take an active part in establishing their learning goals: Together they plan what they will study about a problem that invites genuine inquiry. They form small groups on the basis of common interest in a subtopic and cooperate in carrying out their plan. The plan frequently involves a division of work among group members, so that Group Investigation combines individual, pair, and group study. When they complete their inquiry, groups integrate and summarize their findings. Finally, they decide how to present these findings to their classmates. Throughout the process teachers guide their students in the social and academic skills that make it possible to investigate a topic in groups.

Readers may choose to turn to the different chapters in the book in the order that best suits their needs. Teachers interested in implementing Group Investigation will find the stages of the process clearly spelled out in Chapter 4. Chapters 2 and 3 suggest ways of developing cooperative discussion and planning skills that are essential for carrying out Group Investigation. Detailed examples of actual projects are presented in Chapter 5. These examples demonstrate that the application of Group Investigation is not limited to any one subject or grade level.

Educators interested in the theoretical background of Group Investigation will find in Chapter 1 a comprehensive exposition of the fundamental ideas on which Group Investigation is built. The effectiveness of this method, as demonstrated by research, is presented in Chapter 6. Chapter 7 provides the outline of two series of workshops for teachers who wish to learn Group Investigation. Teachers familiar with other cooperative learning methods will find them mentioned specifically or embedded in the procedures we recommend.

Group Investigation has a long history, although not always in the specific form presented in this book. Throughout the book we acknowledge our indebtedness to our predecessors. Herbert Thelen's work is an inspiration for all who wish to find a way for children and teachers to engage together in an authentic quest for knowledge. Alice Miel, in her pioneering work, showed how cooperative planning can be the basis for such a quest. Bruce Joyce and Marsha Weil's work helped us focus on the structure of group investigation.

Years of creative cooperation with a group of colleagues in Israel gave the process its present form. This group, including Rachel Hertz-Lazarowitz, developed models for teacher training, guided the implementation in classrooms, and studied the effects of Group Investigation. Dina Shemer was a member of the original team that developed Group Investigation, and we are grateful to her for collaborating in the preparation of Chapter 5 of this book. This group joined the International Association for the Study of Cooperation in Education at its inception in 1979, thus beginning an ongoing fruitful exchange with many colleagues in the field of cooperative learning.

We benefited from our association in 1986–1987 with teachers in the Kyrene School District in Arizona, who implemented cooperative learning in diverse and original ways. An earlier version of the workshops for teacher training was prepared together with Michael Lang of the Arizona State Department of Education.

From the moment the writing of this book began, many good friends and colleagues were generous with their time, advice, and encouragement. We especially thank Aviva Davidson (Yael's sister), Ophra Ayalon, Chana Gat, Rachel Gazit, Aharon and Chaya Colodner, and Molly Levine. Mark Brubacher gave us stimulating and helpful suggestions for the project "What Makes a Poem a Poem?" We consulted with Duba Ya'akobi for the preparation of the project "What and How Do Animals Eat?" Richard Schmuck, Nancy Graves, and Ted Graves offered insightful and constructive suggestions for enhancing the clarity of the text.

Mira Friedman is the artist who drew the cartoons, and Micha Bar-On photographed the stamps in Chapter 5. We thank Lea Hermann for typing the manuscript. We especially thank Cathy McClure, editor at Teachers College Press, for her significant contribution towards the clarity and consistency of the text.

The smallest group is a pair. This book is testimony to the cooperative dynamics of a pair at work.

EXPANDING COOPERATIVE LEARNING
THROUGH
GROUP INVESTIGATION

1

Group Investigation: Foundations, Rationale, and Goals

Group Investigation is a method for classroom instruction in which students work collaboratively in small groups to examine, experience, and understand their topic of study. Group Investigation is designed to appeal to all facets of the students' abilities and experience relevant to the process of learning, not just to the cognitive or social domains. It provides educators with an approach to the conduct of teaching and learning in school that differs significantly from traditional instruction. Group Investigation is not simply another technique for improving instruction so that students can learn more at a faster pace while teaching and the classroom environment remain largely as they were. To comprehend fully the goals and meaning of the Group Investigation method, it is imperative to examine the intellectual, pedagogical, and psychological foundations upon which this method is based.

Group Investigation seeks to translate into classroom practice some of the main educational goals and principles formulated by John Dewey (1859–1952), the primary philosopher of education in a democratic society. His work has had a profound and lasting effect on educational thought not only in the United States but in other countries as well. That is not to say that Dewey's ideas are practiced

1

widely in contemporary schools. Unfortunately, like many great thinkers, Dewey seems to be revered more than followed.

In the past few decades, many educators and psychologists have added their insights and contributions to enlarge upon Dewey's basic perspective. Their work allows us to appreciate all the more the depth and breadth of Dewey's grasp of the potential for human development embedded in the educational process. They also provide us with a rich array of possible procedures for implementing Dewey's ideas in today's classrooms. The people who have made noteworthy contributions to the general approach to school learning found in the Group Investigation method include Kurt Lewin, the founder of "group dynamics"; Herbert Thelen, who wrote many inspired works about task-oriented groups in various social settings, including education; the constructivist school of cognitive psychology as reflected in some of the writings of Jean Piaget, Irving Sigel, and others; and, finally, psychologists such as Richard DeCharms and Edward Deci who have developed and studied the theory of intrinsic motivation. These approaches to understanding the multiple dimensions of teaching and learning in school coalesce in the Group Investigation method. Indeed, the inspiration and foundation for the Group Investigation method come from all of these varied sources, alongside the visionary writing of Dewey himself. We will briefly discuss these diverse sources of the Group Investigation method in the following sections of this chapter.

JOHN DEWEY'S PHILOSOPHY OF EDUCATION: SOME BASIC IDEAS

For Dewey, the process of learning in school was, at one and the same time, a series of social, emotional, and intellectual events. It occurs in a social context in which students have cooperative interchanges with their fellow students and in a school whose structure and operation embodies the principles of democratic society. Students' interest in the subjects they study is stimulated by giving them a reasonable measure of responsibility for influencing and directing their work in school. Dewey's view of teaching and learning took into consideration the organizational, social interactive, motivational, and cognitive aspects of the process of schooling. All of these features are outlined in the following passage from Dewey's "The School and Society," first published in 1899:

Almost the only measure for success (i.e. in school) is a competitive one, in the bad sense of that term—a comparison of results in the recitation or in the examination to see which child has succeeded in getting ahead of others in storing up, in accumulating, the maximum of information. So thoroughly is this the prevalent atmosphere that for one child to help another in his task has become a school crime. Where the school work consists in simply learning lessons, mutual assistance, instead of being the most natural form of cooperation and association, becomes a clandestine effort to relieve one's neighbor of his proper duties. Where active work is going on, all this is changed. Helping others, instead of being a form of charity which impoverishes the recipient, is simply an aid in setting free the powers and furthering the impulse of the one helped. A spirit of free communication, of interchange of ideas, suggestions, results, both successes and failures of previous experiences, becomes the dominating note of the recitation. . . . In an informal but all the more pervasive way, school life organizes itself on a social basis. . . .

The great thing to keep in mind, then, regarding the introduction into school of various forms of active occupation, is that through them the entire spirit of the school is renewed. It has a chance to affiliate itself with life, to become the child's habitat, where he learns through directed living, instead of being a place to learn lessons having an abstract and remote reference to some possible living to be done in the future. It gets a chance to be a miniature community, an embryonic society. (Archambault, 1964, pp. 301–303)

Dewey argues that children's experience in school should have a high degree of continuity with life in the adult world, not be set apart and conducted in a manner unrelated to the structure and values of the society. Such continuity is necessary to maintain a democratic society from generation to generation. The means of education should be designed to be essentially related to the goal of having students live as citizens in the society around them. Education should not assume that students understand that school learning is preparation for the life they will live later as adults. Schooling must be deeply meaningful and consistent with students' lives *now* if the values, knowledge, and skills that schools cultivate are to affect students' lives in the future. Education for the future must be compelling in the present, or its message will not survive.

For example, schools generally proclaim that they wish to cultivate the pursuit of knowledge as a value. If so, then school learning should be designed to have students experience the *pursuit* of knowledge. Most frequently, schools present information prepackaged and ready made for the student to acquire *as is*. The students are not given the opportunity to seek out information, discuss and analyze it, understand it, relate it to ideas they have already, and thereby transform this *information* into *knowledge* for themselves. The means schools employ to cultivate *the pursuit of knowledge* as a goal of education are not necessarily appropriate for the goal. Too many students emerge from their years at school unaware of the process of pursuing knowledge as a value that they recognize and with which they have learned to identify.

Furthermore, citizens in a democracy should be able to think critically for themselves as well as be able to exchange ideas and opinions freely with others. Critical thought can be conducted in a social environment that allows for public verification through orderly discussion. It is not developed by teachers' verbal transmission of information that students must master with little or no opportunity to debate its validity, relevance, meaning, and so forth. It is widely acknowledged today that public schooling in its present form is not particularly successful in cultivating students' ability to think critically about knowledge, about themselves, or about their world (Baron & Sternberg, 1987).

Dewey was very much aware of this problem as early as the end of the nineteenth century. He wished to convey the message that schooling should embody in its very procedures the process and goals of democratic society. Citizens in a democracy must participate in determining and clarifying the rules by which they will govern their collective lives. Students in school should be involved together in planning the nature of their school environment and of their process of learning. We cannot cultivate a sense of responsibility for learning and for social living unless we give that responsibility to students, in a manner commensurate with their age and ability. The predominantly verbal and rote methods of teaching and learning typical of traditional instruction deprive students of the opportunity to assume responsibility for what they study. Moreover, the content and method of school learning are more often than not perceived to be dependent on teachers' authority, not on students' decisions! Dewey sought to make students members of a learning community in which knowledge is constructed collaboratively (Wells, Chang, & Maher, 1990). Traditional teaching places students in the role of recipients of information delivered in predetermined quantities, at a pace regulated by the teacher, according to some impression of the median speed with which the class seems able to absorb it. In contrast with students' maturing abilities over their years in school, the higher the grade level in school, the less the independence granted to students to determine the content and method of their study, and the more teachers lecture to them about subject matter dictated by an overburdened curriculum.

What must receive special notice in Dewey's conception of education is its insistence that school learning is not designed to aid the preparation of people who have stored up an arsenal of facts. Nor does it aim at producing scientists or scholars, although we hope that people devoted to these latter goals will emerge from public education. Dewey viewed education as the process of helping cultivate an enlightened society in which people live together in a democratic fashion. Hence Dewey's emphasis on cooperation and the absence from his work of a reliance on competition to ignite students' motivation to excel. Cooperation binds people together; it serves as the cement of social groups. Competition rips groups apart; it atomizes the classroom society and turns it into a collection of individuals, setting people against one another rather than strengthening the social fabric. Competition is the hallmark of an elitist education, not one seeking to cultivate egalitarian values and relationships among peers.

Education should strive to have students acquire a profound sense of belonging to social groups, without losing their individuality, rather than fostering disconnected individualism through competition for artificially limited resources (e.g., to be the "first" one in the class, or the one with the "highest" grade). This view of education seeks to provide as many students as possible with the opportunity to develop their abilities to the fullest and excel in their knowledge and grasp of matters. The message is that excellence need not be realized at someone else's expense.

Group Investigation is a flexible set of guidelines for the design of school learning that organizes the process of study. The goal of this organization is to create conditions that allow students, in collaboration with their classmates, to identify problems, plan together the procedures needed to understand and cope with these problems, collect relevant information, and *cooperatively* (thought not necessarily *collectively*) prepare a report of their work, usually in some creative and interesting way. These steps reflect the stages typical of the scientific method of research regardless of the subject of the investigation. Dewey emphasized this latter point in his essay "Science as Subject Matter and as Method" (Archambault, 1964). The social context of the peer group provides the opportunity for students to examine their information critically in collaboration with others and to reach conclusions, but not necessarily agree with everyone in a conformist fashion.

Dewey also indicated the need to have students become aware of the process by which they direct the gathering and analysis of information, that is, experiencing and understanding the nature of the relationship between reasoning (both inductive and deductive) and the empirical world. School learning should, in Dewey's conception, recapitulate the process whereby knowledge is generated, so that students are partners in that process, not merely consumers (Wells et al., 1990). Involvement in the process of generating knowledge, at the pace and level appropriate for themselves, permits students to perceive that knowledge is related to their own lives. The relationship between the active, self-directed pursuit of knowledge and the grasp of its relationship to one's life, are critical ingredients for the formation of meaning. Forced acquisition of given quantities of information alienates students from identifying with the pursuit of knowledge as a personal value for the conduct of their lives (Archambault, 1964).

Group Investigation is one way to realize Dewey's conception of education in a set of procedures that can be implemented in classrooms without reorganizing the entire school and teaching staff (as Dewey would have wanted). The Group Investigation method makes it possible to achieve some important goals of education without a revolution. Undoubtedly, implementation of Group Investigation requires some distinct changes in current practice. The nature of these changes will become evident as we present the various components of the Group Investigation method.

KURT LEWIN, HERBERT THELEN, AND HUMAN ECOLOGY

A second set of ideas and principles that comprise the basis for the Group Investigation method is the school of group dynamics. One of the most original and central figures who laid the foundation for the social psychology of groups and had a powerful effect on many disciplines (Stivers & Wheelan, 1986) was Kurt Lewin (1890–1947).

Dewey and Lewin never met, but the essential relationship between their fields of interest has been noted by several authors, particularly the concern both men had with the future of democracy:

> Both recognized that each generation must learn democracy anew;
> both saw the importance to social science of freedom of inquiry,

freedom that only a democratic environment could assure. If Dewey could be termed the outstanding philosopher of democracy, Lewin was surely the major theoretician and researcher of democracy among the psychologists. (Schmuck & Schmuck, 1988, p. 3)

Lewin developed the figure of the social engineer who contributed to the effective management of relationships among people participating in some group effort (Lewin, 1947a, 1947b). Vast numbers of people meet daily in organizations of one kind or another in which, almost inevitably, they work in groups, such as committees, work teams, and so forth. It soon became apparent that methods for designing relationships within groups and for improving the effectiveness with which people in groups relate to one another and perform their tasks has enormous potential for developing social organizations. Such organizations include schools and classrooms as well as commercial, industrial, and service institutions.

Equally central to Lewin's work was his general view of human behavior in its social and environmental context. Lewin emphasized the fact that behavior cannot be understood exclusively in terms of an individual's personality. What a person does or says is not just a result of what transpires inside the person. Nor was Lewin thinking in terms of responses to stimuli, as behaviorism taught. For Lewin, to understand behavior it is imperative to consider the social, organizational, and even the physical environment that exerts influence on people. More than any other psychologist of his time, Lewin attributed great significance to the interaction of people with their surroundings as the key to understanding human behavior. The way the entire context in which we move is organized and operated affects what we do and how we do it. Lewin was a psychologist of human social ecology par excellence.

The importance for educational and community life of organizing and managing groups of people who meet to discuss and clarify ideas and plans, and to make decisions or solve problems, was fully grasped and elaborated upon by Herbert Thelen (1954, 1960, 1967, 1981). He forged the link between a Deweyian perspective on school learning and Lewin's social ecology and technology. Thelen combined the view of learning as the conduct of inquiry by students who work together and cooperate in small groups with the theory and method needed for the effective management of groups that solve problems and make decisions in a democratic fashion.

Thelen knew well that people who are about to participate in the work of a small group of their peers have to be prepared for this role and learn basic principles of how to function in a group. It can be counterproductive to ask people, of any age, to cooperate with others in a small group when they have not had any experience with or preparation for functioning in this kind of setting. Thelen suggested an entire plan for the study of academic subjects through the use of cooperative small groups within the classroom setting. In that sense, he was the forerunner of what later became known as cooperative learning.

Thelen employed the distinction made by Hannah Arendt (1958) between *work* and *labor* to present his plan for an investigative approach to learning through peer cooperation in small groups (Thelen, 1967, 1981). Work is the kind of effort made when people try to solve a problem, make judgments and decisions, produce some useful object, or try to cope with a situation that has meaning for them and involves them emotionally. Labor is exerted when people perform a task for reasons external to themselves according to procedures laid down by others for reasons not related to the people performing the task. The laborer is not psychologically involved in the performance of the task to the extent that he or she might wish to ask genuine questions about it. The approach to classroom teaching that Thelen and the Group Investigation method represent

> keeps the child working, not laboring. The elements of this method are that the child purposively contributes skills and ideas to common goals by coordinating his contributions with those of others; the child helps maintain the group as a viable decision-making and communicative medium through which individual goals and contributions can be monitored, assimilated and legitimated by the larger classroom organization; the child finds support . . . and awareness of his own thoughts and feelings through interaction with selected other children in small groups. Activity is purposive and genuinely meaningful. (Thelen, 1981, pp. 114–115)

The writings of Dewey, Lewin, and Thelen should make us sensitive to the fact that students' behavior in school, including how they study, is deeply affected by the way in which we design all the components of the educational setting. Group Investigation, and the methods of cooperative learning in general, seeks to redesign at least the immediate social environment in the classroom. The main elements of classroom teaching and learning that the Group Investigation method considers crucial to its proper implementation include the following:

- The patterns of interaction among individuals in the classroom, including teacher–student and peer interactions
- The way students organize their study in small groups and interact with one another within these groups
- The planning of the study project's topic and goal
- The process of acquiring and examining relevant information
- The use of resources for obtaining information
- The time available to acquire, analyze, discuss, and understand information
- The combining of information from diverse sources into a meaningful whole
- The evaluation of the results of the group effort

All these components comprise the organizational and social context that the Group Investigation method must design in order to make possible the process of meaningful learning in school. When ordered in a manner consistent with the principles and goals of this approach, these components facilitate and stimulate learning. The various components of Group Investigation are discussed in detail in later chapters. In the following sections of this chapter we discuss the relation of Group Investigation to students' intellectual functioning and motivation to learn.

A CONSTRUCTIVIST PSYCHOLOGY OF COGNITION

Schooling concerns, in part, the development of students' knowledge. Schools and teachers organize and carry out the function of teaching on the basis of their concepts of how students develop knowledge. Of course, not each and every school necessarily formulates for itself how the kind of teaching practiced in that school contributes to the development of students' knowledge. Schools are organized and run according to accepted patterns of professional behavior. Yet even if the school does not formulate explicitly the rationale as to why it proceeds with the work of teaching in the way it does, the method of instruction ordinarily employed in a school is based on a set of assumptions about how teaching and learning should take place. These assumptions are always inherent in the pedagogical work of teachers (Sarason, 1982, 1983; Thelen, 1981).

If we look closely at the implementation of instruction in classrooms, what seems to direct a great many teachers is the assumption that students' minds are a tabula rasa upon which the teacher inscribes information. The simile of the mind as an empty vessel into which knowledge is poured is equally appropriate for characterizing schools' and teachers' "theories in use" (Argyris, 1982). These theories are implicit in the kind of instruction practiced in many, perhaps most, classrooms above the third grade (and certainly in secondary schools). The assumption underlying these approaches to teaching implies that knowledge is an impersonal and objective body of information whose existence is unrelated to human subjectivity. Schools are mandated, it is claimed, to transmit this knowledge intact and error-free to the learner. For this purpose, the teacher and the textbook are the primary sources of error-free knowledge, and the pupils' task is to absorb, understand, and demonstrate "mastery" of this information upon demand (Barnes, 1976; Yaakobi & S. Sharan, 1985).

A constructivist psychology of how students acquire knowledge takes quite a different view. This approach was also developed by John Dewey, as well as by the Swiss psychologist Jean Piaget and his disciples (Sigel & Cocking, 1977). Constructivist cognitive psychology asserts that individuals actively build or construct their own notions of reality out of their experience. Gradually, these constructions create broad ideas that constitute knowledge. The fact that a teacher presents information to students, or gets them to read a passage from a textbook, does not transform this information into knowledge from the students' point of view. When people organize pieces of information and use them to build a conception and interpretation of the reality they have experienced, knowledge can then emerge. Knowledge is what people construct out of elements of information, feelings, and experience, not something that exists in chunks in the external world that we imbibe as is, with the requisite amount of repetition. We do not absorb the world; we grab hold of it and take it in:

> The world is not fed to us which we then passively ingest; rather, we ingest it through actively reaching out and taking it in . . . we build a conception of our reality through our experience with it. . . . Participation and engagement in the event are the active bases from which a construction of the particular is developed and from which meaning is extracted, a meaning shared in part with others. (Sigel & Cocking, 1977, p. 226)

Hearing *about* a topic, without any experience with its real manifestations in the world, frequently proves to be an inadequate basis for meaningful learning for a very large percentage of students in school.

Yet, observations of typical classrooms almost anywhere in the Western world unambiguously reflect the fact that teachers are trained to "pour knowledge into" their students, rather than stimulate them to ask questions and to seek ways of solving problems. The in-depth study of instruction in elementary and secondary schools across the United States reported by John Goodlad supports this claim (Goodlad, 1984).

A recent analysis of many teachers' patterns of instruction in elementary schools showed that 24% of the time of a given lesson was occupied by teachers' questions, 18% by teachers' instructions to students about what to do, 20% by discipline (either personal or collective), 9% by lecturing, and all other activities, including student seatwork, recitation, giving praise, and so forth, consumed 29% of class time (Hertz-Lazarowitz & Shachar, 1990).

Who Asks the Questions?

Special study of how frequently students ask questions during classroom lessons has revealed that all the students together in a given classroom ask approximately 2 questions per lesson compared to between 40 or more questions asked by the teacher during the same period (cited in Sarason, 1983, 1990b). Traditional instruction in schools is directed by what the teacher wants the students to know and what the teacher has planned to present. It is not typically directed by what the students may or may not know, understand, or wish to learn about a given topic. Since the flow of information, and even of questions, is primarily from the teacher to the students, the obvious purpose of these questions is not to seek a solution to a problem. Teachers ask questions of students not to obtain an answer that is unknown but to determine whether the students know the answer the teacher considers to be the correct one.

The very same finding about who asks questions in typical classrooms was reported in the massive study by Goodlad. He writes that:

> Students rarely turn things around by asking questions. Nor do teachers often give students a chance to romp with an open-ended question . . . the intellectual terrain is laid out by the teacher. The paths for walking through it are largely predetermined by the teacher. (Goodlad, 1984, p. 109)

Group Investigation seeks to change this typical pattern of classroom principles and procedures and to redefine the teachers' and students' roles. Since teachers have more mature knowledge than the students, they should be *answering* questions, not asking most of them. Since the students are the people in the classroom who are there to study and learn, they should be asking the questions. Moreover, the people doing the studying should define the problem they study and determine the problems of knowledge that must be solved in order to study that topic in a way that makes sense to them.

Interpretation and Knowledge

A genuinely instructive approach to teaching, based on the view just presented, should maximize the students' opportunities

- To learn by asking questions
- To obtain information relevant to these questions
- To interpret this information and their experience

In this fashion, Group Investigation seeks to create conditions that allow students to bring their entire range of personal abilities to bear on topics of study. They are challenged to mold, analyze, and synthesize bodies of information. By so doing they *interpret* the meaning of this information in light of their experience, knowledge, interests, and abilities. Above all, Group Investigation seeks to provide students with the opportunity to *cooperate in interpreting* the meaning of the information they gathered (Barnes, 1976; Thelen, 1981).

Interpretation of information is an important step in transforming information into knowledge. Interpretation is a key element in allowing students to make the content of their study their own mental property. Such an approach would avoid, as much as possible, requiring students to absorb preselected, prepackaged, and previously interpreted information. Interpretation of information by the students is an essential component of the Group Investigation approach to learning, just as asking students to *recollect* on a test what they heard from the teacher or read in the text is intimately related to direct, whole-class instruction. When we orally present information to students, we want to know if they listened and understood what we said. When the students themselves seek information in different sources, we are concerned primarily with knowing if they pieced together, that is, synthesized, the information so as to make sense out of it. This latter effort is interpretation (Wells et al., 1990). Most often, when we have engaged in interpretation of information or experiences, we recall the relevant ideas almost effortlessly, even without repeated review of the material. Not so when we learn topics by listening to a teacher or reading a selection from a text. Memory for material studied in this fashion often requires painstaking effort, which most students, of all ages, do not relish!

We would expect that teachers who conduct their classes with the Group Investigation approach would do so in the spirit of the principles described here. Indeed, teachers in the Group Investigation classes do in fact relate very differently to their students than they do when teaching their classes according to the principles and constraints of the whole-class method. When Hertz-Lazarowitz and Shachar (1990) observed Group Investigation lessons, they found a dramatically different situation from the one found in classes taught with the whole-class method. In the Group Investigation lessons, teachers devoted 11.5% of the time to facilitating communication among students, 28% to helping students conduct their work in groups, 12.5% to encouraging students, 11.5% to giving feedback, and 10.5% to giving praise; 26% of the time was devoted to all other activities. These data reflect how Group Investigation embodies a completely different model of student learning than traditional instruction.

This model of instruction emphasizes student investment in the active search for information by collective action with peers, followed by interpretation of the information in such a way that, eventually, it can become knowledge for the students. Information is found, examined, discussed, molded, interpreted, and summarized by students, albeit with the teacher's help and guidance, but not *by* the teacher. A social and intellectual milieu quite different from the one engendered by the traditional form of instruction has been created. (An excellent description of this process, often through the words of the students themselves, is presented by Wells et al., 1990.)

Group Investigation classes set aside time for the students' search for information. The investigation is conducted according to a plan the students make as part of their cooperative planning in groups. By so doing, they evolve their own cognitive map that sets out where they will go and how they will get there. Information is selected and examined in light of their plan, not just because it was placed before them by an external agent. Moreover, because the search for information encompasses a variety of sources, students must juxtapose different kinds of information and ideas, decide upon their relative merits, and determine how these different sources complement or contradict one another. Students construct some organization or configuration of their ideas that is communicable to their peers in their groups or to other groups in the class. The final product to emerge from the groups' work will most likely reflect some degree of public verification. Hence it will have a greater degree of "objectivity" (Piaget's decentering) than typically will emerge from individual study carried out in isolation from others (Barnes, 1976; Furth, 1969; S. Sharan & Shachar, 1988; Sigel & Cocking, 1977).

Group discussions also provide an arena for the creative use of controversy among students over divergent points of view regarding the topic at hand. Such conflicts can be properly employed within a cooperative learning environment to expand students' social and intellectual horizons. The so-called conflict theory of cognitive development has served as one of the theoretical bases of Group Investigation since its inception (S. Sharan & Y. Sharan, 1976). Recent contributions to this aspect of cooperative learning promise to give "creative conflict" a more prominent role in the practice and study of cooperative learning (Johnson & Johnson, 1988; Johnson, Johnson, & Smith, 1986). Debate among students about ideas contributes to their ability to interpret the information and make meaning of it.

INTRINSIC MOTIVATION TO LEARN

Throughout the development of cooperative learning, its major proponents have consistently emphasized the need to enhance students' motivation to learn. This need is particularly crucial in light of the widespread impression of so many educators and students that traditional instruction stifles motivation (Goodlad, 1984; Sarason, 1983). Indeed, the motivating features of cooperative learning have been given a great deal of attention in the current literature on cooperative learning (Johnson & Johnson, 1985; S. Sharan & Shaulov, 1990; Slavin, 1987). There is, and probably always will be, some controversy over the best ways to motivate students to learn. We will not concern ourselves here with that controversy. Rather, we wish to stress that the Group Investigation approach to cooperative learning seeks to embody the principles and procedures that will attract students' genuine interest in the subject at hand. Our intention is to design the critical features of the learning environment in such a way that it will stimulate and sustain students' interest so they will invest their energy and time in studying various topics out of their own curiosity and desire to learn. Our goal need *not* necessarily be to improve the quantity of information that students can produce on an achievement test, although that may be one effect of using the Group Investigation method, as has been documented by a good deal of research.

Again it was John Dewey who, already in 1899, formulated the basic ideas of intrinsic versus extrinsic motivation to learn in the context of classroom instruction. In his classic book *The School and Society*, Dewey wrote:

> Too often it is assumed that attention can be given directly to any subject-matter, if only the proper will or disposition be at hand, failure being regarded as a sign of willingness or indocility. Lessons in arithmetic, geography, and grammar are put before the child, and he is told to attend in order to learn. But excepting as there is some question, some doubt, present in the mind as a basis for this attention, reflective attention is impossible. If there is sufficient intrinsic interest in the material, there will be direct or spontaneous attention, which is excellent so far as it goes, but which merely of itself does not give power of thought or internal mental control. If there is not an inherent attracting power in the material, then . . . the teacher will either attempt to surround the material with foreign attractiveness, making a bid or offering a bribe [reinforcement!] for attention by "making the lesson interesting"; . . . But, 1. the attention thus gained is never more than partial, or divided; and 2. it always remains dependent upon something external—hence, when the attraction ceases or the pressure lets up, there is little or no gain in inner or intellectual control. And 3. such attention is always for the sake of learning, i.e., *memorizing ready-made answers to possible questions to be put by another.* True, reflective attention, on the other hand, always involves judging, reasoning, deliberation; it means that the child has a *question of his own* and is actively engaged in seeking and selecting relevant material with which to answer it, considering the bearings and relations of this material—the kind of solution it calls for. The problem is one's own; hence also the impetus, the stimulus to attention, is one's own; hence also the training secured is one's own . . . leading the child to realize a problem as his own, so that he is self-induced to attend in order to find out its answer. (Dewey, 1943, pp. 147–149)

A later statement by Dewey succinctly presents his view of motivation:

> Men do not shoot because targets exist, but they set up targets in order that throwing and shooting may be more effective and significant. (Archambault, 1964, p. 72)

In these and in other passages, Dewey identifies the two out-standing features of intrinsic motivation. (1) Individuals consider the goal or activity they wish to pursue as their own, not imposed upon them from without, and they actively pursue ways of reaching the goal or of pursuing the activity. (2) When we are motivated by our own interests, we not only relate and attend to the task at hand; we actually go out to find ways of engaging in the kind of task or activity in which we are interested. We create the opportunities to experience that activity and to work at it (as opposed to laboring over it) rather than just waiting until they come along.

Psychologists have invested much effort in the study of intrinsic motivation. Edward Deci (1975) defined it in terms very similar to those used by Dewey 53 years earlier:

> Intrinsically motivated behaviors will be of two general kinds. When there is no stimulation people will seek it. A person who gets no stimulation will not feel competent and self-determining; he will probably feel "blah." So he seeks out the opportunity to behave in ways which allow him to feel competent and self-determining. He will seek out challenge. The other general kind of intrinsically moti-vated behavior involves conquering challenges. (p. 61)

(For a closely related perspective on intrinsic motivation, see De-Charms, 1968, p. 328).

There is little doubt that students in school most often are prodded to learn by external goals that they do not perceive as stemming from their own questions, curiosity, interests, needs, or life-relevant situations. Moreover, schools employ a range of external rewards and punishment to arouse or maintain students' attention to topics of study. Foremost among the external rewards commonly found in our schools is, of course, the use of grades or marks periodi-cally communicated to parents via report cards. Many educators have bemoaned the fact that secondary schools in particular long ago became "factories for marks" rather than institutions of learning. Public education in many countries seems to have acquiesced to the idea that the perpetual threat of punishment by low grades is the only thing that keeps students' noses to the grindstone (Goodlad, 1984; Sarason, 1983). Schools appear to have given up on trying to provide frequent occasions for intrinsically motivated learning.

Research has shown that external rewards such as marks can actually reduce students' motivation to learn rather than enhance it. Offering rewards for learning something can detract from students' interest and their initiative to study a subject on their own (De-Charms, 1968; Deci, 1975; Piaget, 1973; Ryan, Connell, & Deci, 1985; Weitz & Cameron, 1985). Arousing students' inner motivation to learn requires more pedagogical sophistication than the promise of standard rewards for the amount of information produced on tests. Our position is that we can have classrooms pursue learning with a high level of intrinsic motivation and that it is within our reach to do so.

Arousing Students' Interest

How would teachers design classroom learning in order to try to arouse students' genuine interest in learning? Of course, one cannot overlook the need to make available to students an appropriately rich variety of resources for seeking the information they need to carry out their own group-directed investigations successfully. Some of these materials are to be found outside the school in the community and are not always obtainable in sources that can be easily moved into the school (Sarason, 1983). But beyond the problem of the "learning materials," it should be clear from the cited passages by Dewey, Deci, and others that students must be given the opportunity to exercise a reasonable degree of choice regarding the subject and method of their study. To make choices, they have to be helped to ask their own questions and seek information about the topics they decided to study. The problem that students seek to resolve or cope with must be felt to be related to their own curiosity, experience, ideas, or feelings. Moreover, the norms, procedures, expectations, and relationships among peers in the class must support the endeavor.

Small groups of students that cooperate to identify problems, plan procedures for finding information, discuss their work and findings, and synthesize their individual results to form a group product of some kind provide a practical vehicle for implementing the goals of teaching and learning that we have presented here. Given these conditions, there is every reason to expect that students will become personally interested and involved in studying topics that schools wish to have them learn. The purpose of this book is to present many ways, all subsumed under the title of the Group Investigation method, in which teachers can implement these ideas in their classrooms.

The differences between this approach to arousing student motivation and the methods practiced in too many of our classrooms should be more than obvious. In Goodlad's (1984) nationwide study in the United States it was learned that: "At the elementary level, about 55% of the students reported not participating at all in choosing what they did in class. About two thirds of our secondary students said they did not help make such decisions" (p. 109). Clearly, the enhancement of intrinsic motivation to learn requires a change in our approach to teaching. These changes are described in detail in the following chapters. This book describes an alternative approach in sufficient detail that teachers can implement it in their classrooms.

THE CRITICAL COMPONENTS OF GROUP INVESTIGATION

By proceeding in Dewey's footsteps we can identify four essential components of school learning that typify this approach. These four components can serve as criteria for knowing whether we are implementing the Group Investigation method in keeping with its basic principles and goals, or whether we have merely made some cosmetic changes in the conduct of classroom teaching and learning. Clearly, we cannot expect different results if we continue to employ the old methods. Sarason's (1982; 1990b) message about change in schools is that the more they change, the more they stay the same! That warning should put us on our guard that changes in name alone cannot produce results that are any different from those obtained before.

The four components we consider to be the primary indicators of the Group Investigation method appear in Figure 1.1. In the Group

Figure 1.1   The Four Critical Components of Group Investigation

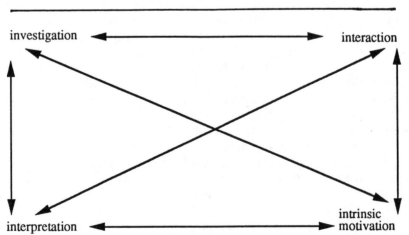

Investigation classroom these four components are interrelated and occur simultaneously. Each component refers to a different dimension or level of implementation of the Group Investigation method.

1. *Investigation* refers to the organization and procedures for directing the conduct of classroom learning as a process of inquiry. It is the most general of the four components in this model, identifying the teacher's and students' orientation toward the process of learning. This orientation of the entire class makes it possible for the other three components of the Group Investigation method to take place.
2. *Interaction* identifies the interpersonal, or social, dimension of the learning process as it unfolds in the communication among members of small groups in the classroom.
3. *Interpretation* occurs both at the interpersonal as well as at the individual cognitive level. The interaction among students in small groups stimulates their individual effort to attribute meaning to the information they have acquired in the process of investigation. Individuals' understanding of the topic under study is enhanced by their interpretation of the information.
4. *Intrinsic motivation* refers to the nature of the students' emotional involvement in the topic they are studying and in the pursuit of the knowledge they seek to acquire. The goal is to have students become personally interested in seeking the information they need in order to understand the topic under study.

The simultaneous combination of all four components is a fundamental feature of the Group Investigation method. In the following chapters we elaborate on how to develop and implement them so that they can be carried out in an integrated fashion.

2

Setting the Stage for Group Investigation

Five students who were investigating Captain Cook's discoveries met to discuss the factors that contributed to his fame. The discussion began with the chairperson's question:

JACK: What is Cook most famous for?

ANN: Well, we know that he's famous for discovering New Zealand and Australia.

EBEN: That's true, but he's also known for not having anyone on his ships die of scurvy.

SONDRA: What's that?

EBEN: Oh, I read about that in an encyclopedia. The sailors got very weak and had bleeding gums because they didn't have any vitamin C . . . no fresh food for a long time.

ADAM: So how did Cook prevent scurvy? How could he keep the food fresh?

EBEN: He gave his sailors sauerkraut and oranges.

JACK: So what do you think? What's more important? That he took care of his men or that he got to Australia?

These students were part of a sixth-grade class carrying out a Group Investigation on explorers. (The full report appears in Chapter 5.) They knew how to interact in a group, how to ask questions and find information relevant to their topic, and how to search for the answers to their problem. How did they develop these abilities? In this chapter and the next we explore some of the many ways teachers can lay the foundations for these cooperative procedures, all of which are implemented in Group Investigation. We suggest ways for establishing the cooperative classroom, for developing interactive talk, and for helping students reflect on the group process. Finally, we stipulate elements of the study task that facilitate cooperation, and we present sample lessons.

DEVELOPING THE COOPERATIVE CLASSROOM

The most basic step in developing cooperative procedures is to have students sit in small groups, but this alone does not insure that they will communicate freely and work well together. If we ask them to change the way they sit in the classroom without helping them change the way they work with one another, we will just confuse them—and ourselves. Although being in a group is not new to children, studying in a group may be new and even strange. Most classroom situations afford children little opportunity to discuss what they are studying, let alone to make choices and decisions. Or the students may be accustomed to being constantly compared to their peers according to criteria determined by teachers. For want of a different model, this attitude may pervade their own interaction in the group, thus obstructing cooperation.

Whatever the reasons, it takes time to create new habits and new expectations, both for the teacher and for the students. Therefore the transition to learning based on interaction among peers should be made gradually. Teachers must slowly redefine their roles as "direct supervisors" to that of facilitators of cooperative learning (Cohen, 1986). With time and practice students gain confidence in their ability to work together. As they strive to change, students and teachers alike will benefit from exercises, activities, and lessons specifically designed to develop the attitudes and skills needed for learning together in small groups.

In recent years, educators have gained a great deal of experience in conducting cooperative learning. They offer teachers clear and well-thought-out guidelines for all aspects of managing the cooperative classroom. They describe and prescribe many different methods for learning cooperatively. In addition, they supply teachers with a stimulating pool of interactive games and activities, among them writing, math, language, and art lessons, which help lay the groundwork for cooperation in the classroom from preschool to high school.

How can all the available guidelines and methods for establishing a cooperative classroom help teachers and students prepare for Group Investigation? Obviously, the central features of cooperative learning serve as a foundation for, and are an integral part of, Group Investigation. All cooperative learning strategies are based to some degree upon a classroom climate that fosters mutual help, that encourages students to work together in small, mixed-ability groups and to exchange materials, ideas, and/or information. Effective interaction in these groups depends partly on the extent to which students have mastered discussion skills, partly on the extent to which the structure of the learning task facilitates cooperation.

We will not attempt to summarize the abundant suggestions available in the professional literature for ways of establishing the cooperative classroom, because the various authors speak very well for themselves. The following sources are but a small sample of what is available to teachers: Adcock and Segal (1983), for example, offer a creative and flexible curriculum guide for the development of cooperative interaction in children aged 3 to 6. Cohen (1986) encourages teachers to systematically prepare their students for cooperation so that all students, including low-status ones, will be full participants in group work. Cohen describes the dramatic change in the teacher's role when conducting group work and makes many helpful suggestions for classroom management. Graves and Graves (1990) have written, edited, and compiled a rich menu of activities to choose from when launching the cooperative classroom. Johnson, Johnson, and Holubec (1986) present basic principles of cooperative learning and suggest many ways of developing collaborative skills. Kagan (1989) presents a wide variety of ways to organize group work in any content area and points out their domains of usefulness. McCabe and Rhoades (1988) and Dishon and O'Leary (1984) specify the many social skills that go into creating a cooperative classroom and provide basic lesson plans. Slavin (1990) and colleagues have developed several student team learning methods that enable students to help one another succeed at learning in groups.

All the suggestions for activities and lessons in the above-mentioned sources provide students and teachers many opportunities for group discussion. Although outwardly an obvious component of the cooperative classroom, the kind of talk that takes place in small groups deserves some further elaboration.

INTERACTIVE TALK IN THE COOPERATIVE CLASSROOM

One of the most characteristic features of the cooperative classroom is that several groups frequently conduct discussions simultaneously in different parts of the room. This is in marked contrast to the traditional classroom, where the teacher is often engaged in the "business of emceeing" (Moffett & Wagner, 1983) and feels obliged to do most of the talking. The traditional teacher may fear that interactive talk distracts students from learning. By contrast, the teacher of the cooperative classroom believes that when students talk among themselves they elaborate on the subject, challenge and amend one another's ideas, and thus remember these ideas more easily.

Teachers are not alone in holding opposing views about the value of talk in the classroom. Some students welcome the opportunity to talk with their classmates about their learning, while others may hesitate and feel insecure. Some may fear that what they say publicly will be labeled "wrong" and that every utterance will be judged in light of the teacher's expectations. This is especially true when students and teachers alike believe that only learning that is constantly mediated by the teacher is "real" learning.

Our understanding of how talk contributes to learning has been enriched by the extensive studies conducted by linguists and educators in the United States as well as in Britain, Canada, and Australia (Barnes, 1976; Britton, 1976; Brubacher & Payne, 1982; Dias, 1990; Forrestal, 1990; Moffett & Wagner, 1983; Wells et al., 1990). Their research and experience offer convincing testimony to the fact that interactive talk is not idle talk. On the contrary, they show that children's talk makes a significant contribution to learning. In these educators' view, talk is not merely a way of conveying existing ideas and knowledge to others. Talk is also a way by which students explore their ideas, clarify them to themselves and to one another, expand and modify them, and, finally, make them their own. If these processes are at the heart of meaningful learning, what better way to promote them than by making small-group discussions a staple part of learning in all subjects and in all grades? Cooperative learning strategies offer teachers ways to organize their classrooms so as to increase the opportunities for unmediated communication among peers.

How can teachers develop productive talk? The success of their efforts depends on two main thrusts, which are the subject of the next two sections: (1) establishing a classroom climate and norms that encourage students to talk together and (2) deliberate development of discussion skills.

Establishing a Climate That Encourages Interactive Talk

Teacher Modeling.   A basic condition for developing a climate receptive to talk is for teachers to set an example for the class in the way they react to students' suggestions, ideas, and opinions. The first rule is to avoid judging and evaluating everything that is said. Students should be encouraged to express their ideas and opinions without the fear of censure. By giving thoughtful consideration to what students say, the teacher creates an atmosphere in which learners have the confidence to say what they think. Such a climate establishes the foundation for the exchange of ideas and opinions that takes place in group work.

Students should also be made to feel that the teachers will listen to their ideas with respect and expect them to listen to one another in the same way. There are two simple ways to do this that do not require any change in classroom organization. One is to praise and reinforce what students say without repeating what was said. Another is to ask other students to react to what a classmate said before the teacher does so. Gradually, less time is allotted to the pervasive interchange between the teacher and one student at a time, which reminds some of a game of Ping-Pong. The teacher's questions and the students' direct answers are no longer the only exchanges that bounce back and forth in the room.

Modifying Teachers' Centrality.   When teachers encourage students to listen to one another, they take the first step in modifying their role as the central focus of attention in the classroom. Even though this small step does not involve a major change in classroom organization or instruction, it is nevertheless very significant. For many teachers it may be the first departure from the belief that their students' success depends on their constant direction and supervision.

In order to ease into this new role, the teacher can design specific situations that encourage students to talk together and exchange ideas or information without his or her direct intervention. Gradually, these situations can increase the amount of time students spend in unsupervised exchanges. With each successive experience students will begin doing many of the things the teacher ordinarily does, "like answering each other's questions, keeping each other engaged in the task, helping each other get started" (Cohen, 1986, p. 96).

Direct talk among students can be introduced in the middle of a teacher-led lesson. The teacher might pose an open-ended question and invite a five-minute exchange of possible answers between pairs of students. The teacher may ask a few students to share with the class what they discussed. Here are some sample questions:

Think of a few ways to make change from a dollar.

Can you find examples to show how Steinbeck lets the reader see events through Jody's eyes?

Why do you think the Mississippi lost some of its importance at the end of the nineteenth century?

Questions like these invite students to share, in a short discussion, their knowledge and understanding of the topic. It is important that at this initial step the teacher not criticize what was said. Instead, he or she should point out how the students' diverse answers can in fact enrich the whole-class lesson. Teachers can incorporate the appropriate answers and ideas into the remainder of the lesson and suggest that the other answers be discussed at a later time.

This strategy, in combination with wait-time, has been refined into a technique called "Think–Pair–Share" (McTighe & Lyman, 1988). It is simple to learn and applicable in all grades and content areas. The steps of "Think–Pair–Share" are:

1. Students listen while the teacher poses a question.
2. Students are given three or more seconds in which to think about their responses (wait-time).
3. Students talk with each other in pairs about their responses.
4. Finally, they share their responses with the whole class. Teachers use cuing devices, such as cards or hand signals, to help the students move smoothly from step to step.

We realize that most teachers at one time or another have posed open-ended questions to students or have asked them to think together about a topic and then report their ideas to the class. Our suggestions are presented here not as self-contained strategies but as a first step in a series of deliberate actions to be taken in order to build a cooperative classroom, all the easier because of their familiarity. When, in the course of a lesson, teachers invite their students to discuss a point among themselves or to exchange ideas or information, they are legitimizing interaction as a vehicle for learning. The message is clear: The teacher is no longer the sole source of knowledge. By interacting with their peers, who have been sitting there all along, students come to view one another as sources of learning and of new ideas rather than as potential competitors for that elusive commodity called "knowledge." The way the teacher interprets and organizes the material under consideration need not be the only way to do so. By designing the lessons to include the various ways the students have come to understand their world, the teacher acknowledges their contribution to the class's learning process. (In the section, Designing Tasks That Facilitate Interactive Learning, we specify how the learning task can be designed so as to incorporate students' ideas.)

A well-kept secret is how much the *teacher* is enriched by hearing what students have to say. The 30-odd people in the classroom may be younger and shorter (in most instances), but they have been busy constructing and reconstructing their worlds all their lives. Surely their experiences are a rich source of potential contributions to classroom learning, for one another as well as for their teachers. Making these experiences a real part of the class's learning promises some unexpected additions to what might otherwise become an all too predictable routine.

When the teacher creates many opportunities for such direct exchanges, students will be more likely to believe that the teacher really means it when he or she invites them to learn by interacting with one another. By his or her own reactions to what students have to say and by encouraging them to talk and listen to one another, the teacher consistently weaves interaction among classmates into the fabric of the regular lesson.

Activities that foster interaction may be *combined with subject matter* even as early as kindergarten. In a kindergarten class we visited, we observed how the children had a chance to talk to one another about the care of pets.

One morning the mother of one of the children brought the family's dog to class. After telling the children about how the family cared for it, she invited them to ask her questions. From their questions it became clear that the children had a great deal of experience with pets. The teacher suggested that they share this experience and introduced a short activity that included practice in listening.

The children paired off at random. They spread out in the room and spent ten minutes "interviewing" each other. Each child asked his or her partner if there was a pet in the house and, if so, how it was cared for.

When the ten minutes were up, the children reconvened as a whole class. Then the teacher asked several children to tell the whole group what they had heard from their partners. She praised each one by saying something such as "You really listened to Sally!" or "You found out a lot by listening to Ben."

The activity lasted a very short time, but it introduced a new element into the classroom: Listening to one another, as they do outside the classroom, is a legitimate activity inside the classroom as well. By listening to one another, students can learn from one another, not only from the teacher. And the teacher heard many ideas she herself had not thought of beforehand.

Developing Discussion Skills

In their short "interviews," the partners in the kindergarten class described above got a taste of the main means of communicating in small groups: Group members discuss their experiences, their ideas, their plans, their opinions, and so forth. At first students may be unsure of what is expected of them, especially if they have experienced only teacher-led discussions. When in groups they may naturally follow the teacher's example and expect one student to dominate the discussion. The transition from the largely passive role of listener and consumer of information to the new, active role of participant may require some practice and reassurance.

Teacher-Led Discussions. The teacher's first step in the development of discussion skills is to apply them in teacher-led, classwide discussions. During the discussion the teacher can demonstrate the skills expected from the students, such as listening, paraphrasing, encouraging participation, concentrating on the topic, and reacting in a nonjudgmental way. It is most important, as we stressed above, that the teacher listen with genuine interest to what the students say. Instead of reacting to and evaluating each statement, the teacher may give more turns to the students. After all, the teacher knows his or her turn will come and can therefore afford to wait and let the students talk.

Teachers' Questions. Classwide discussions are also affected by the questions teachers ask and the way in which they phrase them. Note the difference between these two questions: "What caused the hero to leave town?" and "What might have caused the hero to leave town?" The first question seeks a specific answer that will be judged right or wrong. Some will recall the answer and others will not. The latter question will be more likely to spark a discussion because it invites a wider range of answers. Teachers may then sit back a bit and hear some answers they might not have had in mind. Questions like these also encourage students to bring their own thoughts into the discussion (Adams, 1985; Barnes, 1969).

Questions that involve difficult concepts may have single right answers, but they may require more than factual knowledge in order to arrive at these right answers. Encouraging students to discuss such questions among themselves allows them to generate a variety of approaches to the answer. For example, the study of evolution requires the understanding of the process of adaptation. There are several questions that can help students understand the role of adaptation in the evolution of life on earth, such as "What adaptations have we made to make it easier for us to survive in the water?" or "What did fish need that might cause them to go on land?" (Hassard, 1990). When they search for the answers to questions like these, students grapple directly with the various components of the answers and deepen their appreciation of the concept involved. (For a clear, comprehensive presentation of the role of whole-class and small-group discussions in the classroom see Slavin, 1986, pp. 275–283).

Skill-Building Exercises

Modeling discussion skills and posing questions that draw the students out are essential for establishing new ways of communicating in the class. In addition the teacher can conduct specific skill-building exercises at regular intervals. Let us look at a few sample exercises that promote discussion skills.

Practicing Four Discussion Skills. "The Four-Stage Rocket" (Cohen, 1986, p. 169) is an exercise that teaches pupils four essential skills that enable their group discussion to "take off like a rocket." These skills are conciseness, listening, reflecting (repeating what has been said by the previous speaker), and contributing. The class is taught each skill separately, and then students practice it by conducting a discussion in small groups. The teacher chooses a topic for discussion (with or without any connection to specific subject matter) and the groups proceed as follows:

Stage 1. *Conciseness*—Group members conduct a discussion for five minutes. One student serves as timetaker, making sure that each person talks for only 15 seconds.

Stage 2. *Listening*—The discussion resumes for five more minutes. A new timetaker is selected, again allotting each person only 15 seconds. In addition, each person must

wait 3 seconds after the person before has spoken before taking his or her turn.

Stage 3. *Reflecting*—A third rule is introduced into the discussion: Everyone who speaks must begin by summarizing
in short what was said by the person who spoke before.

Stage 4. *Everyone contributes*—The discussion continues and all
previous rules apply, with the additional rule that no
one may have a second turn until everyone in the group
has spoken at least once.

During each stage of the discussion, student observers note how
well each group does on the skill being practiced. The class uses this
information to assess its progress. This exercise can be repeated at
regular intervals. As groups note that they have mastered one of the
stages, they can repeat the exercise, practicing only the two or three
skills that need refining. Another way to carry out this exercise is to
have groups take turns, one at a time, conducting a discussion, while
all the others serve as observers. Students may also practice each
stage separately.

Naturally the students benefit if group composition remains constant for as long as it takes to practice discussion skills. That way
students do not have to deal with the necessary adjustment to new
groupmates at the same time they are learning new skills.

Reaching Consensus. A less structured discussion exercise is
"The Untitled Story" (Graves & Graves, 1990). In this exercise, all the
students read a rather dramatic story involving several characters.
Afterwards, each one ranks all the characters in the story, from who
is most responsible for the action to who is least responsible. Groups
are formed randomly as individuals finish their ranking. Group
members have to produce one ranking acceptable to all. The only
means they have for doing so is by discussion, and because there
really is no correct ranking, the discussion is often a lively one, as
everyone tries to convince the others that he or she is right. Someone
will inevitably say: "It's so obvious that the Baroness is responsible!"
Each fervently believes that his or her ranking is correct—until con-
fronted with someone else's "correct" ranking!

As he left for a visit to his outlying districts, the jealous Baron
warned his pretty wife: "Do not leave the castle while I am
gone, or I will punish you severely when I return!"

But as the hours passed, the young Baroness grew lonely,

and despite her husband's warning, decided to visit her friend who lived in the countryside nearby.

The castle was located on an island in a wide, fast-flowing river, with a drawbridge linking the island and the land at the narrowest point in the river.

"Surely my husband will not return before dawn," she thought, and ordered her servants to lower the drawbridge and leave it down until she returned.

After spending several pleasant hours with her friend playing music, talking and dancing, the Baroness returned to the drawbridge, only to find it blocked by a madman wildly waving a long and cruel knife.

"Do not attempt to cross this bridge, Baroness, or I will kill you," he raved.

Fearing for her life, the Baroness sought out a boatman on the river, explained her plight to him, and asked him to take her across the river on his boat.

"I will do it, but only if you can pay my fee of five Marks."

"But I have no money with me!" the Baroness protested.

"That is too bad. No money, no ride," the boatman said flatly.

Her fear growing, the Baroness ran back crying to the home of her friend, and after explaining the situation, begged for enough money to pay the boatman his fee.

"I never loan money to anyone," he said, "not even to my best friends. Besides, if you had not disobeyed your husband, this would not have happened."

With dawn approaching and her last resource exhausted, the Baroness returned to the drawbridge, attempted in desperation to cross to the castle, and was slain by the madman.
(Graves & Graves, 1990, p. 451)

The follow-up discussion after this exercise is often just as exciting. Many students (of all ages) become aware for the first time of two hurdles that impede effective group discussion: the difficulty of changing one's position and the difficulty of persuading others of one's point of view. On the other hand, for many participants this exercise becomes a vivid demonstration of how rewarding it is to hear other people's opinions. For junior high and high school students, exercises like "Lost on the Moon" (Stanford & Stanford, 1969) provide additional practice in reaching consensus.

Encouraging Participation. Another exercise that develops discussion skills and arouses enthusiasm is "The Mystery Game" (S. Sharan & Y. Sharan, 1976). Everyone gets a card with a clue to the solution of a murder, and by means of discussion the group solves the mystery. The game can be played by one large group of 22 or simultaneously by two or more groups.

1. All the students are seated in a circle. Stand outside the circle and explain the game as follows: "Today we are going to play a game that will help improve our discussion skills. I am holding a set of clues that will help you solve a murder mystery. If you put all the clues together, you will be able to solve the mystery. You must find the murderer, the weapon, the time of the murder, the place of the murder, and the motive. When you think you know the answers and the group agrees on the solution, let me know. Organize yourselves in any way you feel is appropriate. You may not pass your clues around or show them to anyone else. Please do not leave your seats to walk around. Share all your ideas and clues verbally.

   "Some students can serve as observers and timetakers. The observers can make suggestions about how the group could better organize itself and work faster."
2. Hand out the clues, which have been typed on separate cards.
3. CLUES:
- When he was discovered dead, Mr. Thompson had a bullet hole in his calf and a knife wound in his back.
- Mr. Barton shot at an intruder in his apartment building at midnight.
- Mr. Thompson had virtually wiped out Mr. Barton's business by stealing his customers.
- The elevator operator reported to the police that he saw Mr. Thompson at 12:15 A.M.
- The bullet taken from Mr. Thompson's calf matched the gun owned by Mr. Barton.
- Only one bullet had been fired from Mr. Barton's gun.
- The elevator man said that Mr. Thompson did not seem too badly hurt.
- A knife found in the parking garage had been wiped clean of fingerprints.
- Mrs. Scott had been waiting in the lobby for her husband to get off work.
- The elevator operator went off duty at 12:30 A.M.

- Mr. Thompson's body was found in the park.
- Mr. Thompson's body was found at 1:20 A.M.
- Mr. Thompson had been dead for about an hour when his body was found, according to the medical examiner.
- Mrs. Scott did not see Mr. Thompson leave through the lobby while she was waiting.
- Bloodstains corresponding to Mr. Thompson's blood type were found in the basement parking area.
- Police were unable to locate Mr. Barton after the murder.
- Mr. Thompson's blood type was found on the carpet outside Mr. Barton's apartment.
- There were bloodstains in the elevator.
- Mrs. Scott had been a good friend of Mr. Thompson and had often visited his apartment.
- Mrs. Scott's husband had been jealous of the friendship.
- Mrs. Scott's husband did not appear in the lobby at 12:30 A.M., the end of his normal working hours. She had to return home alone and he arrived later.
- At 12:45 A.M. Mrs. Scott could not find her husband or the family car in the basement parking lot of the apartment building where he worked.

4. ANSWER:

   After receiving a superficial gunshot wound from Mr. Barton, Mr. Thompson stepped on the elevator and was killed by Mr. Scott, the elevator operator, with a knife at 12:30 A.M. because Mr. Scott was jealous.

This game highlights the fact that any and every group member may have information the group can use, regardless of social or academic status. The individual clues ensure that everyone must be heard at least once in order for the group to consider all available information. In the follow-up discussion after the game, students reflect on how they succeeded in solving the mystery. Did they need a chairperson? How was a chairperson chosen? How did the group organize the sharing of the clues? The teacher should point out how important it is to let everyone have a chance to speak so that the group can complete its task.

Like most of the exercises used to build cooperative skills, "The Mystery Game" also serves as a model for the structure of a cooperative learning task. The whole topic (in this case, the mystery) is divided among everyone to ensure maximum participation in the discussion. The distribution of clues also ensures that everyone is supplied with the "material" needed to make a relevant contribution to the discussion (in this case, in order to solve the mystery). Teachers will find more games and activities that are designed to develop discussion skills in Stanford and Stanford (1969).

HELPING STUDENTS REFLECT ON THE GROUP PROCESS

Teachers generally feel pressured to emphasize the academic content of the task at hand and pay less attention to the interpersonal process. By devoting time at the end of a cooperative learning activity to reviewing how they worked together, teachers and students alike can increase their sensitivity to how they are affected by cooperative interaction. Teachers can learn if they are being over- or underdirective. They can also stand back and consider how well students interact and what aspects of interaction need improving. With this information in mind it will be easier for them to set the pace for the future climate—and skill-building activities.

In cooperative learning, how people study together and how they relate to each other influence how well they will accomplish their task. When students listen to one another during a group discussion, for instance, they are not merely being polite. They are facilitating the exchange of ideas necessary for the group to reach an agreement on the topic being discussed. Time spent reviewing how group members worked together increases students' self-awareness of this process. It also makes them feel more in control of the process: They take part in observing their interaction and are not solely dependent on the teacher's evaluation and comments.

Graves and Graves (1990) suggest that reflection include the following components:

- *Identifying* what happened in the session that helped or hindered the group reach its goal. Students may observe that "Today no one interrupted during the discussion," or "Not everyone had a chance to talk."
- *Analyzing* why things happened the way they did and how the group can do things differently next time. "Next time we'll choose a timekeeper to stop us after three minutes so that everybody'll get a turn."
- *Generalizing* how skills learned in this session can be applied in new situations. "It's so nice when everyone listens . . . I guess I'll try to listen more patiently next time we work in groups."

- *Goal setting* for task and group maintenance skills. "Our group has to practice making sure that everyone gets a turn to speak; we'll keep on choosing a timekeeper till we're good at it."

Reflection can be a written or an oral activity. There are several ways of carrying it out:

Each student can write down his or her impressions of the activity and then share them with a partner. Afterwards one pair can share with another, and finally the teacher can lead a whole-class summary.

The teacher may ask the students to relate to any specific aspect of cooperation he or she wishes to reinforce, such as listening to others, encouraging participation, helping others, and so forth.

The students may write down their answers to three questions: What did the group do well together? What needs improvement? How can the group improve the way it works together?

In the lower grades the teacher can present the students with a card that has a happy face and an unhappy one and ask the children to circle the one that shows how they feel about the activity. A follow-up discussion will draw the children out to specify what made them feel the way they did.

DESIGNING TASKS THAT FACILITATE
INTERACTIVE LEARNING

When the teacher asks students to reflect on how they work in groups, he or she helps them understand the *process* of learning cooperatively. When the teacher assigns an appropriately structured task, he or she provides the *means* for learning cooperatively.

It is not necessary to wait for students and teachers fully to master cooperative skills before applying them to academic tasks. As we saw above (p. 26), the development of cooperative skills may easily be integrated with the study of subject matter. In fact, it is helpful to carry out these activities in all content areas, so that cooperative learning will be a thread that runs throughout the schoolday.

Guidelines for Designing an Interactive Learning Task

How can teachers design the learning task so that students interact and exchange their personal experiences and knowledge in the shaping of new knowledge? Three basic guidelines for designing an interactive learning task are followed by sample lessons from various grade levels and subject matter.

The learning task that fosters cooperative interaction should be designed so that:

- Every group member can easily participate.
- The task provides all with an opportunity to talk.
- Group members have to make choices and joint decisions.

Participation.   First and foremost the task must be designed so that every group member can easily participate. One way of facilitating participation is to have students *work in pairs.* Pairs are the most manageable group. Many teachers prefer to have students learn in pairs for as long as it takes them to get used to working together. When students work together in pairs, it is not always necessary to assign each one a specific role. Two learners can share the work quite easily on tasks that call for an exchange of ideas or for sharing resources.

Sample tasks for pairs of students are:

Construct meaningful sentences from separate words.
Fill out a joint chart while observing the habits of the class pet.
Classify material into several categories.
Discuss "what if . . ." and write down your ideas.

Another way to have everyone take part is to assign the group a task that has *two steps.* The first step requires each group member to read, write, or carry out an activity on his or her own. This step gives everyone time to become directly involved in the task and to prepare something to "bring" to the group, and in this way to be individually accountable to the group. In the second step group members combine all individual contributions and build on them to create a joint product. A sample group task for grades 3–5 that includes these two steps is:

1. In small groups the students determine which objects a magnet repels and which objects it attracts. Each group member chooses several objects and then experiments with a magnet to see which objects are attracted and which are repelled. Each student then records his or her findings and pastes the list on the group's poster. The completed poster represents the group's combined findings.

2. Group members discuss their findings with one another to see what conclusions they reach. One group member then records their joint conclusion on their poster.

The Opportunity to Talk.   For reasons we have already clarified, an essential feature of an interactive task is that it provide the students with a forum for informal talk and direct communicaton about what they are studying. The assignment should pose a question that invites more than one answer. As long as there is a basis for genuine joint deliberation—about the arrangement of a sequence of sentences, the different uses of maps, or various interpretations of a story—students' talk will not be limited to the search for the one correct answer or to guessing what the teacher has in mind. A task that promotes interactive talk is one that engages students in sharing their ideas, exchanging and elaborating on information, making choices, and making decisions. As research has shown (Sharan & Shachar, 1988), students are less inhibited in their speech and more willing to express themselves when small group discussions are an integral part of the learning task. This is especially true for less advantaged children (see Chapter 6, Academic Achievement).

Making Choices and Decisions.   When faced with several possible answers or more than one source of information, group members have to make a joint decision about what to choose. Making choices helps students relate what they study and how they study to their own interests and ideas (see Chapter 1, 17–18). Choices can be made in one or more aspects of the assignment: Together students can choose which books to use, how to divide the work, how to summarize and display their findings, and how to report to the class.

When students are new to cooperative learning, the teacher may limit the number of choices available to a group. At first, he or she may give all groups the same alternatives from which to choose. They may all be invited to choose one assignment out of a list of three. Or the teacher may suggest that each group choose the order in which they wish to carry out their assignments. The degree of choice and the number of opportunities for choice naturally increase with practice.

All the above-mentioned features of the cooperative learning task combine to enable group members to create a *group product.* The product reflects the choices they made and the conclusions they reached. Based on what they learned together, group members may write a summary, prepare an oral report or a group drawing, and so forth.

Give-and-take about the ideas and information students have will become natural features of the classroom if the teacher creates a supportive climate, develops the students' discussion skills, and designs tasks that enable them to collaborate and interact.

Sample Lessons

The following sample lessons provided genuine opportunities for students to learn through cooperative interaction in a variety of content areas and grade levels. They progress from relatively simple to increasingly complex interaction and cooperation in learning.

On Becoming a Poet. The following lesson (adapted from McCabe & Rhoades, 1988) took place in an English lesson in grade 2. It demonstrates how two children can create a simple group product based on their individual contributions.

> The students were grouped in pairs and each had a sheet of paper and a pencil so they could create a "poem" together. Each group decided who was to be number 1 and who was to be number 2.
>
> All number 1's were asked to write down their greatest wish. All number 2's were asked to write down their favorite place or activity. When they finished, they read their "poem" to each other. A sample poem was: (1) "I would like to ride on the back of the great white whale . . . (2) eating chocolate cake." They then turned to another pair and read their poems to each other.

The teacher didn't feel that every pair had to report to the whole class, since there was no inherent connection between each pair's work. She invited a few pairs of students to read their poems to the class in order to highlight specifically the diversity of their work. After hearing a few poems, she remarked on how interesting it was to have so many different poems in one class.

From Sentence to Story. The following lesson included several basic elements of interactive learning. A third-grade teacher asked pairs of students to arrange sentences in the way they thought best. In order to do so they had to talk about how to arrange the sentences and explained to each other the reasons for their choice.

> The teacher divided the class randomly into pairs. Each pair was given five strips of oaktag, with a sentence written on each. Their task was to arrange the strips in a sequence that made sense to them. There was more than one correct way to arrange the sentences. Each child read all the sentences silently and then discussed with his or her partner the different ways the sentences could be arranged. When they decided on a specific sequence, they called the teacher to check their work. She asked the partners to explain to her how and why they arranged the sentences as they did. Any corrections necessary were done with the pair of students and not in front of the whole class.

The children had the experience of learning with each other and from one another, creating their own product in the process.

Different Ways of Using Maps.   Another example of the integration of rudimentary cooperative skills in a content area comes from a fifth-grade geography class (adapted from Knapp, Swann, Vogl, S., & Vogl, R., 1986). The study of types of maps combined individual and cooperative procedures in one lesson.

> The teacher told the class that in preparation for their unit about explorers, they were going to investigate different ways of using maps. As an introduction to the unit, she invited the students to share their own experience with maps. Students formed random groups of four. The teacher distributed a package of a variety of maps to each group and a worksheet with four questions. The first two questions were individual ones:
> 1. Look at the different maps in the package. In what way are these maps different?
> 2. In what way are they alike?
> When they finished answering these questions, students compared their answers and compiled one list that stated all the features the maps had in common and how they were different. The third question called for a group discussion:

3. If you were a committee that had to plan a new city park, which map would you use? How many other uses can you think of for the maps in this package?

There followed a lively discussion of how these maps may be used for different purposes: for locating amusement parks, for choosing a good place to build a factory, for finding historical sites, and so forth. The recorders wrote down all the ideas group members mentioned and reported them to the whole class in a teacher-led summing-up.

In this lesson active participation in the initial group discussion was ensured by the fact that each student began with his or her own list of answers, which literally gave them something to say. In addition, the questions did not require a particular, predetermined answer. By pooling their ideas, group members created a group product and contributed to the whole class discussion.

Writing Questions. A fourth-grade math lesson (adapted from Burns, 1987) provides an example of how individual and group work combined to encourage children to listen to one another and exchange ideas in order to make sense of word problems.

The teacher wrote the following information on the board:
　　Pencils cost two for $.25.
　　Erasers cost $.10 each.
　　Bill has $1.00.
She asked the children to do three things:
1. On your own, write a question that can be answered from the information posted.
2. In your groups, read your questions aloud, discussing whether they can be answered.
3. In your groups, brainstorm as many questions as you can that can be answered from the same information. Write them on one sheet.
The students worked for twenty minutes. Then the teacher invited them to share a few of their questions with the whole class. She asked that the children listen carefully to all the questions to see if they are the same or different. One student from each group read from the paper they had prepared. Children commented on the similarities and differences among the questions they heard.

After the first round of questions the teacher gave the class a new purpose for listening: "Think about whether it's possible to answer each of the questions from the information you have." This next round of questions aroused many reactions. For homework each child was asked to solve the problems his or her group had written. The following day, in their groups, students compared the answers they had written. The teacher asked each group to think about which types of problems were easy to solve and which were difficult. In a teacher-led discussion, the class summarized those features they considered difficult and those they considered easy.

Individual, group, and whole-class work were mixed in this lesson in order to offer students several ways to stimulate and complement each other's thoughts and ideas. Interacting in these diverse ways helped them make sense of word problems.

The Connection between Jobs and Population. Interactive learning is particularly appropriate for social studies, where learners can share information and ideas based on their experiences outside the classroom. The following lessons (adapted from Knapp et al., 1986) were part of a unit on the history of the community. A seventh-grade class set out to study the connection between changes in the local population and the types of jobs held in the community. After the initial individual step, the students worked in groups of four.

The teacher introduced the activity by saying that the class's inquiry into the topic would begin "at home": Each student would interview his or her family and write down the answers to these questions:
How long has each family been in town?
Where did they come from?
What country did their ancestors come from?
What kind of jobs did they have in other towns
or countries?
What kind of jobs do they have now?
The next day students formed groups of four. They compiled the information they had gathered, and each group prepared a chart that summarized the places the people they had interviewed came from, how long they had lived in town, the jobs they held when they came, and the kinds of jobs they hold

now. All charts were photocopied and distributed to each of the other groups.

In the next social studies period the teacher asked each foursome to spend ten minutes discussing two questions: "Based on the information you have gathered, how has the population of our town changed over time? How have jobs changed over time?" In each group one student recorded all the answers.

The teacher then asked each group to give some thought to another question, in preparation for a whole class summarizing discussion: "You have all compiled a great deal of information. What can you learn from it about the relationship between types of jobs held in town over time and changes in the population?" The teacher reminded the students to refer to all the charts before deciding on their answers. Fifteen minutes were allotted to this step.

After the class heard one representative from each group report the group's answer, the teacher led a classwide summarizing discussion about similarities and differences among the various answers. In her final remarks she integrated the many opinions that students had expressed. She pointed out how together they had learned how the town's population and job patterns were intertwined.

This lesson illustrates how cooperative learning can proceed in a series of steps, where one step lays the foundation for the next. Group members began their inquiry into the topic by gathering information from the source closest to them—their families. They used this information to create a group product—a chart. All the charts then served as the basis for an intergroup "product": an evaluation of all the available information. Finally, the class as a whole had a chance to relate to the different ways each group interpreted the material.

The Structure and Function of a Cell. A tenth-grade biology teacher wanted his students to be active participants in the investigation of a scientific problem (adapted from Adams, 1985).

The teacher posed the following problem: "How does cell structure relate to function?" The aim of the lesson was to familiarize students with the broad range of cell and tissue characteristics and have them consider how these characteristics

are related to function. The students were asked to work in pairs. Each pair was given the same set of ten prepared slides of different plant and animal cells and tissues. The slides were numbered, but not identified by name. The assignment was to:
Observe the cells or tissues on the slide.
Draw the cells or tissue (each student draws in his or her notebook).
Together, speculate about the possible functions of each cell or tissue that you see.
Write your hypotheses as well as your reasons for them.
When the students were ready, the teacher initiated the classwide discussion by projecting each of the slide images on the wall. He identified the organisms and told the class where in each organism the cells came from. He then invited different pairs of students to report their hypotheses as well as the reasons behind them. At this stage of the unit on cell structure the teacher did not tell the class the "correct" answers. He preferred to stress that the "correct" answers are those that make the most sense, given the present evidence. The classwide discussion concluded with the students suggesting what additional evidence might be needed to support or refute their hypotheses.

Exploring the Themes of a Story.   A tenth-grade English class had finished reading the story "The Split Cherry Tree" by Jesse Stuart. There are three main characters in the story: the father, a farmer; his son Dave, a high school student; and the biology teacher. Each one represents a different generation and a different view of the value of education.

The teacher decided to offer the class a choice of three topics for group discussion of the main theme of the story. He introduced the lesson by saying that he would like the class to explore in depth the different ways the author illustrates the generation gap. He distributed a list of topics and asked each group to decide on one. The topics were:
1. "Lettin' you leave your books and galavant over th' hills." That's how education looks to the father. What is Dave's view of education? And the professor's view? Discuss how these different views reflect the generation gap between them.
2. "... I was hunting dry timothy grass to put in an incubator and raise some protozoa." Professor Herbert speaks like that. The father speaks quite differently. Can you infer how Dave speaks?

Discuss how their language reflects the differences in their age and education.

3. "Pa will whip me . . ." "You are too big to whip and I have to punish you for climbing up in that cherry tree." What are the different ideas about punishment found in the story? Discuss how they reflect the generation gap between the father, the teacher, and the son.

The groups spent 20 minutes discussing their chosen topics. Each group chose a recorder, who wrote a short summary of the discussion. When the teacher reconvened the whole class, each recorder read his group's summary.

In order to conclude the discussion the teacher posed a new question for the whole class to consider: "Why do you think the author used the characters' language, their approach to punishment, and their ideas about education to illustrate the generation gap?"

At first students based their answers on the particular aspect of the generation gap that they had explored. As the discussion unfolded they began to see which features these aspects had in common. Students cited evidence from the story for their views but soon began to inject examples from their own lives. This gave the teacher an idea that he had not thought of before, and in the next English period he told the students: "We have explored how the author of this story presents the generation gap. Do you feel that there is a generation gap between you and your parents' generation? Between you and your teachers? Share your experiences with each other and choose a way to illustrate them."

Students returned to their groups and shared their personal experiences with their groupmates. They then decided how they would present their conclusions to the rest of the class. Some planned a short role-play of a conversation among parents, children, and teachers. One group represented their findings as a huge cartoon, drawn on a large piece of butcher paper divided into six squares. Each square depicted one group member's personal experience of the generation gap. The sixth square showed how they all—students and their "adversaries"—met to form their own "AGE" group: All Generations Equal.

Finally, the teacher asked the class to reflect on how they felt about working together. Some students said that going over the story together made it clearer for them. Most students mentioned that they particularly enjoyed sharing their own experiences of the generation gap.

The groups who puzzled over the relationship between cell structure and function, those who explored the theme of a story, those who sought the connection between jobs and population growth in their community ... all of them experienced the stimulation and involvement that comes from learning by interacting with others. Many of the questions and answers (albeit sometimes tentative) in these sample activities and lessons were generated directly by the interaction among students. Talking together, thinking together, and figuring things out together contributed to their learning.

The lessons presented above demonstrate a few of the diverse ways of organizing learning in small groups. They all supply a genuine reason for two or more students to meet in order to study together. Each lesson is structured so that students can share with their peers what they think, know, or feel about a topic. The task highlights and is often based on group members' different backgrounds, values, and abilities. These are indeed the group's greatest asset. The very differences between personalities contribute a wide range of knowledge and skills to the group's work on the task they share.

HOW TO COMPOSE GROUPS

The assumption that everybody is a valuable member of the small group underlies our having advocated *random* grouping, which encourages students to discover what anyone and everyone in their class can contribute to their learning. Random grouping may be based on seating arrangements, so that two, three, or four children sitting near one another work together and become a small group. Other times group formation may be based on *friendship* or on shared *interest* in a particular topic. Students who want to work together or are interested in the same topic will often work together effectively. Small groups may also be formed on the basis of *teacher selection*, to insure that no one is left out for social, academic, or racial reasons.

Since each classroom is a miniature society with its own unique composition, how to form small groups is a challenge teachers face anew every year. There are no hard-and-fast rules to be followed every time. In order to make a reasonable decision regarding group composition, however, there are three major factors to consider:

students' individual characteristics, the nature of the task, and the duration of the group.

1. *The individual characteristics of the students*, such as gender, interests, ethnic identity, skills, and abilities, are highly visible in group work. By observing their students in groups, teachers have an opportunity to learn a great deal about them. They can use this knowledge to assign students to the group in which they may best use their unique talents for their own satisfaction as well as for the benefit of the group (Miel, 1952).

Students who show leadership qualities or those who have had experience in cooperative learning may help a group function effectively. The teacher should not rely on these students to assume these roles permanently, however. As part of the development of cooperative learning skills, the teacher should provide frequent opportunities for all students to alternate between membership and leadership roles (Cohen, 1986; Miel, 1952).

2. *The nature of the task* is another factor to be considered when forming groups. For a highly structured skill-building task, the teacher may want to select group members according to relevant social or academic criteria. As students gain practice in working together, the study task increases in complexity and with it, the composition of the group. When the task is multidimensional and requires a variety of skills, knowledge, and abilities for completion, group composition should reflect this diversity (Cohen, 1986; Miller & Harrington, 1990). A student should not be assigned to a group on the basis of the expectation that as a member of a particular social or ethnic group or gender he or she will succeed (or fail) at a particular task.

3. *The duration of the group* is the third factor to be weighed when deciding on the composition of the group. Some educators feel that group composition should remain constant for as long as it takes the group to acquire basic communication skills and develop a sense of group cohesion. These groups should meet regularly under the teacher's direct guidance. At the same time, groups formed on the basis of interest may meet to discuss a particular topic or carry out a short-term assignment (Moffett & Wagner, 1983). Others feel that the experience of pairing off with as many other classmates as possible at the beginning of the year creates a base for successful group work later. Teachers may choose to have long-term groups in one subject and short-term groups in another (Graves & Graves, 1990; Robertson, 1990).

There is no one formula for composing groups in the classroom. The teacher has to take the above factors into account, as well as the students' reactions to their placement. As we know, their reactions are not totally predictable, and therefore teachers must be prepared to modify their decision if necessary. As the developer of cooperative learning skills in the classroom, the teacher constantly has to negotiate group composition with the students, so that it meets both the teacher's goals and the students' needs. To this end groups will sometimes be composed by the teacher and other times by students' choice or at random.

All the sample exercises, activities, lessons, and considerations presented in this chapter for developing cooperative learning in groups set the stage for Group Investigation. The interactive skills indicated thus far are all used in Group Investigation. But there is one more skill that students should acquire before starting a Group Investigation project. That skill is *cooperative planning*, which is a critical component of the Group Investigation model. In Chapter 3 we present various ways of developing the procedures of cooperative planning that students will use throughout a Group Investigation project.

3

Cooperative Planning

Central to Group Investigation is the plan of the inquiry that the students prepare cooperatively. Cooperation in planning the group's task is a part of each stage of the inquiry, as we describe in Chapter 4. At each phase of the investigation students plan for a different purpose. Yet at all stages of the investigation their planning is based on the deliberate preparation of a sequence of actions that will help them achieve their goals. The cooperative preparation of future action has cognitive, motivational, and social aspects to it, which we discuss in the first part of this chapter.

Planning, like all other skills, can and should be developed gradually and systematically. In the second part of this chapter we set forth a series of activities geared to developing planning skills. We also demonstrate how the development of planning skills may be incorporated into regular lessons in all grades and in all content areas.

But first let us briefly examine the basic characteristics of cooperative planning.

COGNITIVE, MOTIVATIONAL, AND SOCIAL FEATURES OF COOPERATIVE PLANNING

At all stages of Group Investigation cooperative planning has a cognitive, a motivational, and a social dimension. Although they occur concurrently, it is worthwhile describing them separately.

The Cognitive Dimension

Anticipating. One basic feature of cooperative planning is that students anticipate what they will study in the near future. They prepare the questions they will seek to answer. Their questions are not aimed at proving how much they can recall but at expressing what they want to know. Obviously, knowledge acquired earlier serves as a foundation for the investigation of new topics, but at the outset the complete scope of the investigation is unknown. It is impossible to prescribe the exact components of knowledge that the students will acquire as a result of their inquiry. Anticipating what they will study infuses the class with an air of expectation for the outcome of their efforts.

Asking Questions.   Asking questions, so much a part of learning in every child's early years, is unjustifiably stifled in school (Sarason, 1990a). Cooperative planning provides a renewed opportunity for students to ask questions as a natural part of their learning process.

The teacher introduces the general topic for investigation and asks the students what aspect of the topic puzzles them or seems particularly interesting to them. The students are encouraged to ask what they want to know. Their questions form the foundation on which the entire Group Investigation project is based. After this general introduction, each student lists his or her own set of questions. Students then compare their questions with one another's, and the process of mutual enrichment begins. One student's question may spark someone else's interest in the same issue. Or a student may rephrase his or her question after hearing another's formulation. Often a student's interest in a particular aspect of the topic is reinforced by hearing several classmates ask similar questions. Even hearing a question that presents a different point of view can be productive; it often stimulates new avenues of investigation.

At later stages of cooperative planning, students ask: How will we find out what we want to know? Whom can we ask? Where can we get more information? What are the main ideas to be summarized? What is the best way to tell the class about what we learned?

Thinking Strategies.   While identifying the questions that will determine the direction and contents of their inquiry, students employ a variety of critical thinking skills. Not all questions are acceptable, and some must be set aside for a different time. Others may be discarded. As they sift through their questions, they have to evaluate their relevance to their specific subtopic.

In the course of the investigation students search in a variety of sources for the best answers they can find to the questions they asked. The teacher points out the need to frequently check the relationship between the questions they asked and the information they gather. Does the material in fact provide adequate answers to their questions? Is it relevant? Maybe the students will discover that some questions cannot be answered or were not formulated properly. It may happen that some of the original questions must be changed in light of the information obtained during the search for answers.

As group members search for resources, they have to evaluate whether, and how, each source can help them reach their specific goal. They evaluate the information they gather and consider its connection to their initial questions. Sometimes they encounter material that stimulates new questions they had not thought of before. As they proceed with their investigation, students pool their information, after which they draw conclusions about the problem they investigated. Finally, they integrate all their findings into a coherent whole and design a meaningful way in which to transmit it to their classmates.

The Motivational Dimension

Cooperative planning motivates students to take an active role in determining what and how they will learn. It allows them to make individual and joint choices and decisions. They choose the topic they will investigate; they choose the books they will use; they decide how they will interview a resource person; they determine which sites they will visit and whether or not a particular TV program will be helpful. They decide whether they will prepare an exhibit of their findings for the class or whether they will put on a short skit.

In effect, they write a "script" that determines their behavior over the course of the investigation. The guidelines they set are the ones they act upon, thus giving them a great deal of control over their learning. Cooperative planning gives them a chance to exercise responsibility and self-direction in their learning. For a while they share in initiating events in their lives in school and are therefore willing to invest greater effort in learning than when they are constantly told how and what to learn (Ryan et al., 1985; S. Sharan & Shaulov, 1990).

The Social Dimension

Cooperative planning of a common goal draws its motivating power as well as its content from the interaction among group members. While planning their work together, students communicate freely and directly with one another. Many an idea is hatched as a result of hearing what others have to say. Anyone who has participated in a cooperative planning discussion knows how exciting it is to begin the planning session with one idea and end up with so many new ideas that you did not think of before. It is equally gratifying to see how your ideas contribute to others. Cooperative learning is based on shared responsibility and interaction among group members. Cooperative planning in particular provides an excellent opportunity to capitalize on the drive and increased positive interdependence that develop when pupils learn together.

All these dimensions of cooperative planning are interrelated and often occur simultaneously. They combine social and intellectual processes that develop and improve with practice and teacher guidance. In that sense, when developing cooperative planning teachers should follow one of the basic principles of sound teaching practice: Begin with short-term assignments and proceed at a pace comfortable for the teacher as well as for the students. The systematic integration of elements of cooperative planning in their work allows both students and teachers to gradually adopt them as an additional method of learning and teaching.

Teachers and students should look upon their initial attempts at cooperative planning as opportunities for growth in their ability to plan and work together. When teachers offer their classes opportunities for genuine cooperative planning, growth is likely to occur. The examples that appear later in this chapter are designed to demonstrate how cooperative planning can make a significant contribution to the learning experience.

Doubtlessly there is some "risk" involved in having the students plan an activity or a part of a study unit. They may not always come up with plans that concur with the teacher's opinion. The teacher, as the leader of the class, should point out certain considerations that students may have overlooked. On the other hand, the teacher must be careful to respect the students' suggestions. Maintaining the correct balance between what the teacher thinks is appropriate and what the students offer requires the teacher to exercise constant judgment. Too much guidance on the teacher's part may turn into stifling interference; too little may result in a frustrating muddle. We should remember that children engage in a great deal of spontaneous planning outside of school, as when they plan game strategies or some social event (Pea, 1982). With judicious guidance they will be able to apply this ability to learning situations in school.

DEVELOPING COOPERATIVE PLANNING

Cooperative planning can be developed and practiced gradually with the whole class, with pairs of students, and in small groups. There are several ways of doing this at various grade levels, with different subject matter, and for different lengths of time. The purpose of many of the sample assignments in this chapter is to practice one or more features of cooperative planning as part of the ongoing learning activities in the classroom. Cooperative planning procedures are the focal point of the following examples, but other cooperative behaviors are incorporated as well. While engaged in cooperative planning, students also put to use all the communication and collaborative skills that they acquire in other cooperative tasks: They discuss their plans with each other; they exchange ideas and information; and they help one another carry out the assignment.

Learning How to Plan

Teachers can provide many opportunities for their students to learn cooperative planning procedures. The following five ways of developing cooperative planning may be carried out separately or sequentially:

- Plan nonacademic classroom activities.
- Plan how to find information.
- Plan a learning activity.
- Plan which questions to ask.
- Have one group plan for the rest of the class.

Planning Classroom Activities. A helpful way to introduce cooperative planning is to invite students to participate actively and genuinely in deciding what goes on in their classroom. By conducting classwide planning sessions, the teacher takes the first step in creating the climate in which cooperative planning will thrive. Although the teacher is clearly in charge, he or she shares authority with the students.

The teacher's prime responsibility in classwide planning sessions is to encourage participation and show the class that their suggestions are welcome. After posing a question to the class—such as "What should we plan for the next parents' night?" or "How should we store our art work?"—the teacher should listen to all contributions without instantly evaluating them. It gives the students time to think about what they want to say and to get used to the idea that they do the talking. Nevertheless, it may be necessary to point out that a particular suggestion is irrelevant or has already been mentioned. Why not preface such a reminder with a positive remark, such as "That's a good suggestion, Mark; how about adding it to what Ruth already said?"

The teacher can conduct discussions with the whole class for the purpose of planning any aspect of classroom life (Miel, 1952). He or she can invite the students' collaboration by asking, "How can we arrange the desks for the policeman's visit?" or "What questions should we ask the policeman?" Some other questions that elicit suggestions for class activities are:

How should we care for the class' pet or plants?
What should be the agenda for the student council meeting?
How can we exhibit what we learned in this unit?
What kind of menu should we plan for our class trip?

Participation in planning classroom activities sets the stage for planning academic assignments. Part of planning a study task calls for the location of resource materials, which we discuss next.

Planning How to Find Information.   Students need practice in planning how to locate sources of information and resource materials. A sample exercise (adapted from S. Sharan & Hertz-Lazarowitz, 1978) calls for each student to list where he or she would get the information needed in order to:

Plan a visit to a friend in a different city.
Plan a visit to Washington, D.C.
Find the capital of Venezuela.
Find out where his or her ancestors came from.

After each student lists all his or her ideas, the teacher invites them to share them with the whole class. The suggestions are summarized on a chart posted for easy reference (see Table 3.1). It serves as a useful reminder of the many sources they can turn to.

This exercise can be prepared in connection with the study of any content area. With each repetition of the experience, the number of resources grows. The list of sites, for example, may expand to include items such as public buildings and even cemeteries, where a great deal of historical information can be obtained.

Table 3.1 Where Can We Find Information?

PEOPLE	SITES	BOOKS	OTHER MATERIAL
our families	travel agents	encyclopedia	timetables
ourselves	libraries	textbooks	maps
experts	embassies	biographies	photographs
teachers	factories		videotapes
librarians	stores		magazines
			stamps

Additional experience in planning where to find resource material can be gained in a classwide discussion in preparation for the study of a specific topic. In the following excerpt, the teacher encourages her sixth-grade class to seek a variety of sources for their study of space exploration.

TEACHER: Our science text has a lot of information, but perhaps we can also look elsewhere for material.

STUDENT: How about an encyclopedia?

STUDENT: Or science magazine . . .

TEACHER: Can you be more specific?

STUDENT: Well, we could go to the library and look for material . . . the librarian will help us.

TEACHER: That's a good idea; then you could bring the list of books and magazines back to the class. Any other ideas?

STUDENT: My brother has a book on popular science; I'll look in there . . .

TEACHER: So far you've suggested books. How about other sources? For instance, I know that there are two movies on space in the school library, and I'll bring them to class. Let's see what information we can get from them.

STUDENT: Why not write to NASA? Maybe they have movies, or maybe they'd send us a poster.

STUDENT: Yeah, I remember, when I went to Meteor Crater with my family we bought a few posters from NASA . . . maybe I'll find them and bring them.

STUDENT: Maybe we could ask NASA to give us the name of

one of the astronauts who might come and talk
to us.

TEACHER: It's certainly a good idea to write to them and ask
them what kind of material they offer and if they
can recommend a speaker.

Since this was the class's first experience in planning of this kind,
the teacher did not hesitate to step in from time to time with suggestions of her own. All the suggestions were posted on the board under
the title "Where Can We Find Out About Exploring Space?" The
teacher divided the class into committees. Each committee was responsible for getting materials from one of the sources on the list.

Planning a Learning Activity.   Planning a study task requires
students to be able to set their learning goals and articulate what they
want to find or learn as a result of their search. Teachers can help
them specify what they want to look for, even if their planning begins
spontaneously and with little formal organization, as in the following
example.

A second-grade class took a walk in a field in order to observe
signs of autumn. The teacher did not give them any particular
instructions. A few children collected different colored leaves,
while others picked up twigs of different sizes and shapes.
Some dug in the ground and found roots and insects. When
they returned to class, the teacher found a way to highlight the
fact that the children, on their own, had formed groups based
on their common interests. She gave each group a piece of
oaktag. Each group planned how to arrange their "finds" on
the oaktag. The results were hung on the wall for "instant dec-
oration."

No doubt many teachers have seen their students plan an activity
on their own. However pleasant the experience, it remains a marginal
event unless it is reinforced and repeated, so that it becomes an
integral part of life in the classroom. In preparation for the next walk,
the teacher helped the class plan their search.

The teacher asked the children to form groups of four and
asked each group to plan what it would look for. Some groups
decided that each member would look for colored leaves and
wild flowers; another group decided to see what insects they

could find under rocks; and yet another group planned to find squirrels and see what they ate. One child in each group wrote down the group's plan on a strip of paper and posted it on the wall:

THINGS WE WILL LOOK FOR
Group 1. We will look for leaves and flowers.
Group 2. We will look for squirrels.
Group 3. We will see what's under the rocks.
Group 4. We will look for colored leaves.

When they returned to class, the teacher asked each group to decide how it would share with the class what they had found. Some groups arranged displays of the leaves and flowers they had collected. The group that looked for insects drew what they had seen. Although the group that set out to find squirrels only met up with one, they wrote a short description of its antics.

Finally, the teacher reviewed with the class how each group organized its work. She outlined the main points on a chart that she hung next to the groups' original plans:

HOW WE PLANNED OUR WALK
1. We decided what to look for in the field.
2. We went out to find it.
3. We came back to class and shared what we found.

These two vignettes illustrate how in one class the teacher turned an unplanned occasion into an experience in cooperative planning. She facilitated the children's ability to plan by showing them how to organize each step. Similar planning discussions took place a month later when the class was studying a unit on dinosaurs. The teacher asked the children what they would look for on their visit to the local museum of natural history. Their suggestions were listed on a chart and posted on the wall. When they returned from the museum, they discussed what they had seen and compared their experience to the items on the chart. With practice, planning academic and nonacademic activities became an integral part of this classroom's routine.

One imaginative kindergarten class planned a wedding between Mr. Q and Ms. U (Barbieri, 1988). The children listed all the things they needed for the wedding. Then they thought about what they were going to do and wrote their plan on the bulletin board under the heading "Steps in Our Plan." They also listed problems that might spoil their plan. As a result of this engaging activity, the children learned the Q-U relationship and, at the same time, learned how to plan a classroom event.

Another opportunity to plan occurred in a fourth-grade class before a trip to the local museum to see an exhibit about robots. The teacher led the class in a planning discussion and summarized their suggestions on a chart:

WHAT WILL WE DO IN THE MUSEUM?
Take a guided tour of the exhibit.
Find written information on how robots work.
Find pictures of different kinds of robots.
See demonstrations of how robots work.
Write down new words and terms that we need to know.
Buy souvenirs that we can bring back to class.

The discussion served as a reminder of the many possible benefits of the trip and helped focus the students' attention during their visit. Unfortunately, no printed material was distributed at the museum and the class had to plan where to find an alternative source of written information.

Planning Which Questions to Ask.   The teacher asks, "What would you like to know about . . . ?" Students are encouraged to ask those questions about a topic that are of major interest to them. Unfortunately, when in school many children become inhibited about expressing their interests in the form of questions. Students may not be used to asking their own questions in class and may need the teacher's guidance, as in the following example.

Before teaching a unit on desert animals, the teacher asked her fourth-grade class what they would like to learn about these animals. The teacher accepted each and every question that the children contributed, and it was not long before the list grew to more than 30 items. The teacher then tried to help one student phrase her question clearly:
STUDENT: Water . . .
TEACHER: Can you explain a bit more?
STUDENT: Different places . . . where they get it . . .
TEACHER: Do you want to ask if there are different places, not in the desert, where they get water?

STUDENT: No, I mean are there some places in the desert where animals can get water?

The teacher also encouraged other children to express their interest in the subject. She turned to those children who seemed a bit hesitant: "David, on your trip with your family to the desert, did you see any animals? Is there anything you would like to know about them?" "Naomi, what would you like to know about the snake you saw in your backyard?" Teachers can facilitate the process of asking questions by leading whole-class discussions as well as by encouraging individual students (Miel, 1952; Wells et al., 1990).

Formulating questions may also be practiced in pairs, creating an "anticipatory set" for the topic to be studied. The teacher can have pairs of students write down what they want to know about a very specific topic in preparation for a class lesson. The teacher posts all the questions in the students' own words, so he or she can refer to them in the course of the lesson. In this way the teacher reinforces the connection between the students' questions and the topic.

An effective aid is the "Q-Dial," designed to help students formulate their questions (Wiederhold, 1991). This is a tagboard dial with nine question "prompters," such as: Who might? What can? How might? Who would? Why would? Where would? Who will? Why will? How will? Group members take turns spinning the dial. When the dial lands on a word-pair, the student writes it down and then thinks of a question that begins with that word-pair. A typical session with the Q-Dial may proceed as follows (adapted from Wiederhold, 1991):

Four students meet in order to generate questions based on the topic "What Can Be Done to Save Endangered Species?" Susan spins a colored dial and it lands on the word-pair "What can?" She writes it down and passes the Q-Dial to Larry, who gets the words "Where would?" from his spin. As Larry passes the dial to Kemp, Susan thinks for a few minutes and then writes her first question: "What can be done to stop the killing of whales?" By the time the dial gets to Mara, Larry has written his question: "Where would a whale hide?" The dial goes around two or three times, and then the children discuss their questions with one another. When they feel the need for more background material, they check their science text for additional information. By the end of the period, the group has a full list of questions to pursue.

After several attempts to generate questions with the help of the Q-Dial, the teacher may ask each group to try to *sort* their questions into categories. The group above, for example, may combine their questions into two categories: (1) What can people do to save endangered species? (2) How does nature help endangered species? Teacher-led class discussions can also help students sort their questions into categories. These categories become the subtopics that groups will investigate.

Having One Group Plan for the Whole Class.   Another way to introduce cooperative planning is to have one group perform a special service for the rest of the class. Four or five students plan how to carry out an assignment on behalf of the others. If possible, members of the small group should be chosen by the class, rather than by the teacher, as their representatives. When they finish their task, they report to the whole class (Miel, 1952).

The assignment the small group carries out can vary in complexity according to the topic and the students' ages. Here are some suggestions for activities one small group can carry out for the large group:

One group can visit a library, a post office, or any other site to gather information for the rest of the class. This task is appropriate when it is impossible for the whole class to make the trip. Group members plan what to investigate at the site and report their findings to the class.

One group can plan a class party. The group can organize the details itself or decide on procedures and then distribute assignments to their classmates.

As part of a teacher-led unit, one group can plan an interview with an expert on the topic and report the results to the class.

The whole class can suggest poems or songs for a party. They then select a few children to plan a detailed program based on these suggestions.

A task whereby a small group gathered information for the class and also practiced asking questions was the assignment a teacher planned for her third grade. The teacher divided her class into four groups who visited community facilities. Each group had a turn serving as information gatherers for the rest of the class. In addition, each student had a chance to practice formulating questions about what he or she wanted to find out on the visit. The teacher organized the project in the following way (adapted from Miel, 1952):

> The teacher chose four institutions that were willing to host a small group of children: the library, city hall, the courthouse, and the post office. Each site was listed on a chart on the bulletin board. Anyone who had a question about a site wrote it on a piece of paper and tacked it on the appropriate chart.
>
> The teacher divided the class into four committees, one for each site. The committee was responsible for getting the answers to the questions on the list for that site. Each committee examined the questions on their list. They checked to see whether there were some questions that were not relevant. They also checked to see if any questions appeared more than once. When they felt their list was ready, they asked the teacher to check it. They divided the questions among themselves and decided who would ask which question during the visit.
>
> While one group went on the trip with the teacher, the rest of the class was in the charge of another teacher. At each site committee members interviewed their hosts and took turns asking the questions their classmates had listed. They wrote down the answers.
>
> When they returned to school, each group pooled its answers and compiled a report. The children's reports were a bit schematic—the questions and their answers appeared side by side. The reports were posted on the chart under the name of the facility so that each child could come up and read the answers to his or her questions.
>
> At the end of the week the teacher conducted a whole-class discussion to summarize what the class had learned about the four institutions in the community. She then compiled the reports into a file for the school library. A representative of each group wrote a thank-you letter to the people who guided the tour of the facility.

In each of the above examples, the members of the small group gained experience in one or more features of cooperative planning. They planned their assignment, made decisions, searched for information, and reported their findings. It is advisable for each class member to participate in such a group assignment at least once before carrying out more complex cooperative planning. It is important that at this early stage the teacher guide each group in its planning and remind them that all members should participate.

COOPERATIVE PLANNING OF A STUDY TASK

All content areas offer opportunities, great or small, for students to plan some aspects of their learning in pairs or in small groups. Frequent practice will make the students comfortable with their new responsibility for learning. The teacher may then introduce more elaborate planning of a study task, giving small groups more responsibility for the direction of their study.

All Groups Plan the Same Assignment

When the teacher feels that the students have had adequate practice in planning as a class as well as in separate small groups, the whole class can be subdivided into several small groups or pairs. The topic, determined by the teacher, should be relatively easy so that all the groups, working simultaneously, can complete the task in one or two periods, as in the following two examples. In task 1 all groups planned a summing up of their study of the Constitution. In task 2 the students were asked to plan an experiment.

Task 1: What is Most Important About the Constitution?
After having taught a unit on the Constitution to his fifth grade, the teacher divided the class into random groups for a summarizing activity.

> The teacher asked each group to discuss what they considered most important in the Constitution and to plan a poster that illustrated the combined opinions of members of the group. He reminded the class that "Each group member's feeling [about the Constitution] must be represented."
> At first students seemed a bit hesitant. Some checked the section on the Constitution in their textbooks; others ventured a few tentative statements. The teacher did not intervene, and gradually the conversations in the groups grew more animated. Within ten minutes most groups had determined what each member thought most important about the Constitution. They planned their posters and began drawing. The teacher went over to those groups in need of further encouragement. All this

activity resulted in posters that reflected each group's unique responses to the Constitution.

The posters were hung on the wall, and a representative of each group explained its product to the class. Everyone was struck by the diversity and originality of the display. When the teacher asked the class what they liked most about the lesson, many children said that they enjoyed talking about their own ideas and feeling about the Constitution. Some said that there was too much noise in the class, so the teacher elicited suggestions for creating a quieter environment.

Task 2: Planning a Biology Experiment.   A tenth-grade biology class was asked to find out "What gas do growing yeast cells produce?" (adapted from Adams, 1985).

The class was shown the apparatus for growing yeast. The teacher also described how a BTB (Bromo Thymol Blue) solution can be used to indicate the production of gas by changing color. Then the teacher asked the students to form pairs. He handed each pair a worksheet with the following instructions:
1. Speculate what gas yeast may produce. Write down your ideas.
2. Plan at least three experiments that will test your ideas. Your experiments should test the effect of the
    Presence of light
    Presence of sugar
    Presence of air
3. The experiments may take more than one day. When color changes have clearly occurred, record your results and observe some of the growing yeast under a microscope. Write a descriptive statement about what you observe. Record the results of your experiments. Don't forget to mention original conditions, original color, and final color. Post your results on the board.

The teacher circulated among the pairs of students in order to help out when needed. As students completed their experiments, they posted their results and read what other pairs had done. In the classwide lesson that followed these experiments, the teacher led a discussion about the general trend the data produced. He introduced the term *cellular respiration* and the formula: sugar + air → CO. In the next lesson the teacher referred to all the reports on the board and pointed out that not all the experiments had produced the same results. This led to a discussion of the difference between controlled and uncontrolled experiments. The teacher helped students establish guidelines for planning the design of subsequent experiments.

The students in this biology class carried out their work according to some of the fundamental principles of scientific inquiry: They generated hypotheses, tested predictions, planned and conducted controlled experiments, and analyzed the data. The social stimulation of planning and working with a partner enhanced the intellectual stimulation of the scientific inquiry.

Groups Plan Different Assignments

The teachers in each of the following examples gave their students different degrees of choice. In both classes, each student chose which subtopic to investigate and groups were formed accordingly. Although in task 3 the subtopics for investigation were determined by the teacher, the students generated their own questions and planned their presentations. In task 4 the teacher presented a general topic to the class. Students designed the subtopics for inquiry and divided their work among members of the group.

Task 3: Architecture, Engineering, and Language in Ancient Rome. A sixth-grade history class was learning about ancient Rome. In several whole-class lessons the teacher taught about the development of the Roman empire. Three lessons were set aside to explore how the Roman Empire influenced Western architecture, engineering, and language. The teacher felt that the students were ready to deal directly with this question in small groups.

The three topics were written on the board and the students signed up for the topic of their choice. Several groups were formed to explore each topic.

GROUPS PLAN WHAT AND HOW TO STUDY
One group member went to a table where the teacher had placed a collection of source materials and took what was relevant for the group's topic. Then groups looked over the material and spent about ten minutes generating the questions they would attempt to answer. The recorder in each group wrote down all the questions on a large piece of paper, which remained in the middle of the table.

When the list of questions was ready, group members divided the materials among themselves and each one looked up the relevant information. (All the students looked up information pertinent to all questions.) From time to time students turned to the teacher for help. She circulated around the room, ready to assist those who needed help in locating material, formulating a question, or deciding which was the best answer to their questions. She often "answered" their questions by pointing out to them how they could find the answers on their own.

Toward the end of the second lesson, the members of each group pooled all the information they had collected and answered the questions on their list. They summarized their findings in writing. They also planned how they would present their findings to the class. The teacher encouraged each group to vary their written reports in some way that would be interesting and appealing.

GROUPS PRESENT THEIR FINDINGS

For the third lesson the class reconvened as a whole. A representative of each group read the group's summary. (Five minutes were allotted to each group.) In addition to their written summary, the groups that had explored architecture showed pictures of Roman arches, temples, and amphitheaters found in different European countries. One of the groups that had read about Roman engineering explained how amphitheaters were constructed. Another group explained that Roman roads were so well built that some are still in use today. One group that had studied language distributed a list of English words derived from Latin roots. A short exchange in Latin was presented by a second "language group."

THE TEACHER'S WRAP-UP

When all the groups had completed their reports, the teacher posed a question that sought to integrate the three aspects of Rome's influence on the Western world. She wrote two words on the board: *capitol* and *capital.* Then she projected a slide of the Capitol and told the class: "Let's see an example of the influence of Rome in the United States. Here is the *Capitol* building in the *capital* city of Washington, D.C. In what way do the building and the words *capitol* and *capital* reflect the influence of ancient Rome?"

The answers came easily as the students related their readings to the design and structure of the Capitol and to the Latin root of both words.

In this short-term investigation, each group had the opportunity to plan its own questions and seek the answers from more than one source. Each group drew its own conclusions and planned how to share them with the class. The teacher capped the activity by presenting the entire class with an opportunity to apply their knowledge to a new question.

Task 4: Understanding Weather. In the following example fourth-grade students planned what and how to study about the weather.

Before teaching about the seasons to her science class, the teacher explained: "The earth has a variety of seasons due to changes in the weather. Before we understand why we have seasons, we have to learn about weather." She asked them to think about what they wanted to learn about weather. A few children raised their hands and asked such questions as: "What makes weather? Is there the same weather all over the planet? How does the weather change from season to season?" As interest in the topic grew, she asked the class to continue their planning by dividing up into pairs.

ASKING QUESTIONS
In pairs the children generated more questions about the weather. As the teacher moved around the room, she heard such questions as: "Where does the wind come from? How come we hear thunder after lightning? What makes clouds? How do we know what the weather will be next week? How can we tell how much rain fell? Do days become longer in spring?" Some pairs began discussing possible answers to their questions and attempted to clarify basic terms.

TIM: You need sun to make weather.
ROBIN: And air, right?
TIM: Is there air on the moon? Does the moon have weather?
ROBIN: There's no air on the moon.
TIM: But there's sun.
ROBIN: The moon gets light from the sun, so does it have weather?
TIM: Let's write that down: Does the moon have weather?

At the end of the first period, each pair had a list of several questions.

SORTING THE QUESTIONS

The next science period began with each pair of students sharing their list with another pair. Each pair read its list to the other in order to come up with one combined list. The discussion of their combined questions often led to adding new ones that had not been listed before.

When all groups indicated that their lists were ready, the teacher asked them to try to sort their questions into separate categories. She collected the sorted lists and checked them to see how many categories there were altogether. Two categories were phrased differently but seemed to be essentially the same, so she combined them into one. At the next science class she presented each category on a separate placard with all the relevant questions underneath. There were five categories: (1) what makes weather? (2) forecasting weather, (3) weather in different seasons, (4) the dangers of weather, and (5) weather in other parts of the country.

SEARCHING FOR ANSWERS

Students signed up for the group of their choice. There were 15 children interested in forecasting weather, so the teacher divided them into three groups of five. She supplied all the groups with directions for conducting two experiments; one was required and the other, elective. In addition, each group consulted the class science text and a few commercial books on weather in order to answer their questions.

Groups spent two class periods investigating the topic of their choice. In the first period, every group conducted the required experiment. A recorder in each group wrote down their findings.

At the beginning of the second period, each group discussed how they would divide the work: Some children contributed to the investigation by reading and others, by conducting the elective experiment.

SUMMARIZING THE FINDINGS

In the third period each group discussed all its findings and attempted to summarize them and formulate conclusions. The teacher suggested that they write their answers to each and every question on their list and then decide what they could conclude about their topic. In order to make it a bit easier, she also suggested that each topic be turned into a question. Thus "The dangers of weather," for instance, became "What are the dangers of weather?"

TIM: Well, we have a list of all the dangers: hurricanes, hailstorms, lightning . . .

LYNN: Hurricanes are storms that begin in tropical waters . . .

ROBIN: We can make a table of each kind of storm and what causes it.

LYNN: Let's add how each kind of storm is dangerous.

TIM: Should we write down how to protect ourselves from the danger?

SILVIO: Why not leave that for the report to the class?

TIM: Do we know enough about that?

SILVIO: Let's look in _____ [he named a book]

The teacher stopped by and asked how they were doing. The group told her of their dilemma. She suggested that they finish the table first and then look up ways to protect people and homes from storms.

The fourth period was devoted to each group's *report.* Even though three groups had inquired into the ways in which weather is forecasted, the teacher helped each one emphasize a different aspect of the topic.

THE FINAL ACTIVITY

In this unit the final activity was a class visit to a meteorological station. Their guide showed them instruments that the students had not seen in their text and explained their uses.

When asked how they liked this way of studying a subject, the students remarked that they had learned a great deal on their own and enjoyed working on topics they had selected. They pointed out that their science text did not have as much interesting information as the other books they used. They decided that next time they planned a topic they would not present only written reports and would look for more interesting ways to share what they had learned.

Who Plans the Study Task?

The assignments in this chapter demonstrate some of the many ways teachers and students can gain experience in carrying out one

Table 3.2   Who Plans the Study Task?

FEATURES OF COOPERATIVE PLANNING	TASK 1	TASK 2	TASK 3	TASK 4
a. Who determines group composition?	T	S	S	S
b. Who generates the questions to be studied?	S	T	S	S
c. Who sorts the questions into subtopics?	S	S	T	S,T
d. Who supplies resource materials?	T	T	T	T,S
e. Who assigns roles?	S	-	-	S
f. Who plans type of presentation?	T	T	S	S
g. Who plans content of presentation?	S	S	S	S
TOTAL	4 S's 3 T's	3 S's 3 T's	4 S's 2 T's	7 S's 2 T's

or more features of cooperative planning. Table 3.2 lists the last four tasks and shows, in each case, which features of cooperative planning were contributed by the *teachers* and which were considered to be most appropriate for the *students* to plan.

In each task the teacher and students shared responsibility for planning what was to be studied, although not necessarily in equal amounts. Teachers consistently took upon themselves the responsibility of supplying resource materials. In task 4, however, the students also assumed responsibility for that aspect of planning.

In all four tasks the students had the major responsibility for planning the content of the final presentation. This was so even in tasks 2 and 3, where the teachers and the students had equal shares in determining the content of the study task. Planning the content of the presentation is the one feature of a cooperative study task that is always carried out by the students. It is the product of the joint choices and decisions they made as to what they should study and how to go about it.

In respect to the five remaining features of cooperative planning, both teacher and students contributed to some extent to the process of planning. When we look at the columns in Table 3.2 from top to bottom, we see that in task 4 the students carried out independently almost all of the components of planning, whereas in the three preceding tasks the teacher played a larger role in this process. Although the students in task 4 planned all seven elements, that does not indicate that they must do so in all future tasks. Their next task, for instance, may be carried out in one period and only require cooperative planning of the subtopics to be studied.

The list of seven basic features of cooperative planning can serve as a checklist for teachers to use in their own planning. When planning an assignment, the teacher can check off those features of the task for which students will be responsible and those features for which he or she will be responsible. The checklist will make it easy for the teacher to see if the students are in fact getting enough opportunities to practice every feature of cooperative planning. There is no specific, predetermined sequence by which these different components should be introduced into the classroom and practiced. It remains the teacher's responsibility to incorporate those features of cooperative planning that are best suited to the amount of time available, the level of the students' planning skills, and the nature of the study task.

The Stages of
Group Investigation

How does Group Investigation proceed so that students will take an active part in planning what they will study and how they will study? In this chapter we present the stages of Group Investigation and show how they enable students to investigate topics and interpret the information they acquire. Stage by stage, we examine how Group Investigation combines the students' personal worlds and their intellectual curiosity with social interaction with their peers. Let us first see how teachers can prepare for Group Investigation.

TEACHER PREPARATION

The teacher has a critical role in organizing and coordinating the investigation. Most often he or she is the one who initiates the Group Investigation project, determines the timeframe, and provides the materials and initial stimuli for the students' inquiry. During the investigation he or she is the facilitator of the process, helping the students at every stage, as we describe below. There are a number of ways to prepare for this role:

• Acquaint yourself with several sources of information and ideas about the general topic so that you understand the central issues it involves. This will enable you to see the connection between the students' attempts at formulating questions and the key concepts of the broad topic.

- Find out precisely what kind of help is available in the class's textbook, local libraries, museums, and other appropriate sites. If possible, visit one of the sites or discuss the topic with an expert. Be ready to suggest these resources to the class.
- List questions that come to mind as you scan the sources and talk about the general topic with experts or colleagues. Imagine what is involved in investigating each of these questions. This will make it easier for you to help your students formulate their plans.
- Choose a stimulating problem to present to the class. Of all the questions that arise as you explore the general problem, which is the one most likely to generate broad inquiry? Which problem will have the broadest appeal to your students?
- Bring as many materials to the class as you can so as to engage the students' interest in the topic.

Preparing in this way for a group investigation project obviously deepens the teacher's understanding of the subject. It also provides him or her with a broad base for understanding the students' probings of the subject. The teacher may not be equipped to answer *every* question, and indeed that is not his or her responsibility. But the teacher is equipped to appreciate students' questions and help them in their search for answers (Thelen, 1981).

Extensive preparation also makes it possible for the teacher to choose appropriate opportunities for pointing out the relationship between the various parts of the investigation. This may be done in the course of the investigation, after the presentations, and at the evaluation stage.

Throughout the investigation the teacher's role is one of consultant, coach, evaluator, and coordinator. However, at the onset of the investigation it is appropriate to spell out exactly what is expected of the students. The class may be unfamiliar with the social and academic aspects of Group Investigation and will benefit from hearing a clear statement about how the project will be carried out and what the criteria for evaluation will be. The students should be told why they are conducting a Group Investigation project. They should also be reminded that they are partners in the process of ongoing evaluation and at all times are welcome to express any concerns they may have (see stage VI).

It may take some time before the students can carry out an elaborate project. At first it is advisable to conduct short-term investigations on a narrow range of topics (Joyce & Weil, 1986). In Chapters

1 and 2 we explore the many ways the teacher can prepare a class for cooperative investigation.

Another factor the teacher has to consider is how the Group Investigation project fits in with the rest of the curriculum. There may be many components of the larger unit, of which the Group Investigation project is a part, that do not lend themselves to cooperative inquiry. These can be taught by direct whole-class instruction, individualized instruction in learning centers, other cooperative learning methods, or any combination of methods. The central point to keep in mind is that Group Investigation be reserved for that aspect of the general content area that stimulates genuine investigation.

THE STAGES OF GROUP INVESTIGATION

In planning and carrying out Group Investigation, students progress through a series of six consecutive stages, as shown in Figure 4.1.

Classroom Organization

As they proceed from stage to stage, students move back and forth among whole-class planning, individual study, group planning, and group study. At first the teacher stimulates the whole class's interest in a broad, general problem. Each student chooses a part of the problem that he or she would like to investigate, and groups are formed according to common interest in a subtopic. All group members take part in planning how to research their subtopic. In order to carry out their research, they divide the work among themselves. The students move again to an individual phase as each group member investigates what most interests him or her. Students return to the group in order to integrate and summarize their findings. Finally, group members present these findings in some cohesive form to their classmates so that they can see how all the subtopics relate to the general problem. Thus the investigation ends with the whole class acting as a "group of groups" (Joyce & Weil, 1986; Miel, 1952; S. Sharan & Hertz-Lazarowitz, 1980; Y. Sharan & S. Sharan, 1990; Thelen, 1981).

Before we examine the procedures for each stage, as well as the teacher's and students' roles, we would like to point out that they are not meant to be followed mechanically. Teachers can design different

Figure 4.1   Stages of Implementation of Group Investigation

Stage I: Class determines subtopics and organizes into research groups

Students scan sources, propose questions, and sort them into categories. The categories become subtopics. Students join the group studying the subtopic of their choice.

Stage II: Groups plan their investigations

Group members plan their investigation cooperatively; they decide what they will investigate, how they will go about it and how they will divide the work among themselves.

Stage III: Groups carry out their investigations

Group members gather, organize, and analyze information from several sources. They pool their findings and form conclusions. Group members discuss their work in progress in order to exchange ideas and information, and to expand, clarify, and integrate them.

Stage IV: Groups plan their presentations

Group members determine the main idea of their investigation. They plan how to present their findings. Group representatives meet as a steering committee to coordinate plans for final presentation to class.

Stage V: Groups make their presentations

Presentations are made to the class in a variety of forms. The audience evaluates the clarity and appeal of each presentation.

Stage VI: Teacher and students evaluate their projects

Students share feedback about their investigations and about their affective experiences. Teachers and students collaborate to evaluate individual, group, and classwide learning. Evaluation includes assessment of higher level thinking processes.

---

ways of implementing this basic outline of steps, as shown in the four detailed examples of Group Investigation projects in Chapter 5. Additional examples are vividly illustrated in case studies of group investigation projects in environmental studies in elementary schools (Harris & Evans, 1972) and in English and government high school classes (Huhtala & Coughlin, 1991).

Stage I: Class Determines Subtopics and Organizes into Research Groups

This is a classwide exploratory stage with four steps and may take two or three class periods. The four steps are: presenting the general problem; classwide cooperative planning; sorting the questions into subtopics; and forming interest groups.

The teacher has two responsibilities at this stage:

1. To present a broad problem to the whole class
2. To stimulate interest in investigating the problem

Step 1: Presenting the General Problem. The topic may be part of the curriculum, or it may stem from students' interest or from a timely issue. It is best to phrase the topic as a problem rather than as a general statement. Instead of announcing that we are going to study "space exploration," the teacher may present a problem, such as "What is the importance of exploring space?" or "What progress has been made in space exploration in the last 20 years?" Instead of presenting the topic "Arizona Indians," it is better to ask, "What is the history of Arizona Indians?" or "In what ways do Arizona Indians differ from Indians in other states?"

Phrasing the topic as a question serves two purposes. First, it sets the tone for further inquiry. Second, it defines somewhat the scope of the investigation and guides the students in their questions. The problem should be a multifaceted one so that it will trigger a variety of reactions from the students. It should be clear that there is more than one answer and/or more than one source where they can search for the answers.

Posing the question will obviously not be enough to stimulate students' interest in inquiring into the topic. Inquiry may be further stimulated by having the students scan a variety of sources. One or two class hours may be spent looking at films or browsing through texts, picture books, magazines, and so forth. These might be displayed on a table for a week so that they are available to the students whenever they have free time. Perhaps a lecture on the subject would be appropriate, or a visit to a particular site. Viewing a film or hearing a lecture that presents a controversial issue related to the topic may also stimulate the students' interest.

The books, magazines, lecture, film, or visits are intended to help the students begin to see what is familiar to them about the problem as well as what is unknown to them. As students look through the material or attend to a lecture with no prior instructions, they are free to react to the impressions the material makes on them. Does it connect in any way to present or past experience? Does it arouse any feelings? Can they begin to consider any particular aspect of the topic that they would like to explore? Do they find something they have "always" wanted to understand? In fact, the one instruction the teacher may offer along with all the references is, "Look through all this material and think about what you know about it and what you'd like to know about it."

Step 2: Classwide Cooperative Planning. Now the students are ready to formulate and select various questions for inquiry. The teacher writes the general problem on the board and asks, "Now that you've looked at some of the materials that deal with this problem, what do you think you want to investigate in order to understand it better?" Some students will ask questions based on something they have read; others may ask questions related to some of their past experiences. Some questions may relate to broad aspects of the problem, others to a very specific issue. Everyone will participate if the teacher encourages diverse reactions. Remember, at this stage the students are not expected to show what they know but what they *want* to know!

The selection of the various possible subtopics is done by cooperative planning, which can proceed in one of three ways (Gorman, 1969; Miel, 1952; S. Sharan & Y. Sharan, 1976):

- *Individually.* Each student raises questions that he or she would like to investigate. Working alone allows students to think about what it is that captivates them most about the topic. There is no set number of questions that they must produce. After about 15 or 20 minutes, the teacher invites students to tell the class what they wrote and writes each suggestion on the board. As they hear other ideas, some students may add one or two suggestions or modify their original questions.
- *Buzz groups.* Students meet in groups of four or five and take turns voicing their ideas about what to investigate. Students may react to the ideas they hear, but there is no need for consensus. Recorders in each group write down each idea and then report them to the whole class. If the class is small, the teacher may write all the suggestions on the board. Otherwise the teacher collects the groups' lists and compiles one list for the whole class to consider.

• *Individuals, pairs, quartets.* This procedure allows for students to think on their own as well as to exchange their thoughts with others and thus expand or modify them. Planning begins with each student writing down his or her questions. Subsequently it continues in progressively larger groups, from pairs to quartets or even to groups of eight. At each step students compare their lists and compile a single list. The final list represents the interests of all participants.

Step 3: Sorting Questions into Subtopics. The next step is to make all the questions available to the whole class. This can be done by writing them on the board or on newsprint hung on the wall, or by mimeographing them and distributing a copy to each student. The list of accumulated questions becomes the class's "capital—a form of wealth which carries with it a mounting expectation of further interesting investments" (Thelen, 1981, p. 153).

When each student can see all the questions, the next step is to classify them into several categories. This can be done by one of the three methods outlined in step 2. The categories are then presented as the subtopics for separate groups to investigate.

For example, the sixth-grade class that was preparing to investigate "What is the importance of exploring space?" sorted their list of questions into the following categories:

What does it take to be an astronaut?
What can we learn from those who lived in space?
How will our future be affected by space exploration?
How is space explored?
What does space exploration teach us about our planet?

Step 4: Forming Interest Groups. In the final step of stage 1, the titles of the subtopics are presented to the whole class, usually on the board. The result of their planning is thus tangibly displayed before the class. Now each student signs up to investigate the subtopic that reflects his or her interest. Groups are formed based on students' common commitment to investigate the subtopic of their choice.

The teacher may wish to limit the number of students in a group to four or five. If one particular subtopic is very popular, it is possible to form two or more groups that will investigate it. If the subsequent investigation will indeed reflect the combined interests of all group members, then each group will produce a unique product.

Teacher's Role. In this stage the teacher is both leader and facilitator. As the *leader* of this exploratory stage, the teacher encourages students to express different interests and points of view. It is important that he or she not impose suggestions but instead help the students determine the components of the investigation by stimulating student questions, not rejecting them.

As the *facilitator* of the investigation, the teacher may point out and explain which questions are more related to the problem and which would best be investigated at another opportunity. Yet it is important to keep such guidance to a minimum. The teacher's main role at this stage is to facilitate the students' growing awareness of what interests them most about the topic and what they want to investigate.

It might well be that at the first attempt at Group Investigation the invitation to inquiry will yield few questions. In fact, some children may need time to overcome the shock of being asked to say what they want to know about a topic as opposed to what they are supposed to know. If the teacher accepts even a small number of reactions and uses them as the basis for carrying out all the stages, however limited their content, he or she is keeping the implied promise to base the inquiry on the students' questions. No doubt the students will be encouraged to be more forthcoming when given the opportunity to plan again.

Students' Roles. At this stage students have the opportunity to express their individual interests and to exchange ideas and opinions with their classmates. Each student has a chance to discover what interests him or her most about the general topic as well as what interests others. Individually and cooperatively, students generate questions, sort them into categories, and determine the subtopics that will be investigated. Finally, students choose the subtopic they would like to investigate and form groups according to common interests.

The interaction among students during this stage establishes their active participation in making choices and decisions that determine the components of their investigation. If two classrooms undertook to investigate the same general topic and had ample time to generate their questions, we assume that the resulting subtopics would not be identical. Each class would plan subtopics that would reflect the unique interests and choices of the members of that class.

Stage II: Groups Plan Their Investigations

Upon joining their respective research groups, students focus their attention on the subtopic of their choice. Each group has to devote an hour or two to planning its investigation. At this stage group members determine the aspect of the subtopic each one will investigate, singly or in pairs. Members have to decide how to proceed and which resources they will need in order to carry out their investigation.

Group members discuss their views and ideas about the scope of their inquiry. They refer to the list of questions generated by the class in stage 1 and choose those questions they feel best reflect their interest and are most relevant to their subtopic. As the discussion proceeds they add a few questions, reject a few, and so clarify exactly what it is they want to investigate. The five students in the following example were figuring out what they wanted to investigate about their subtopic, which was "How did Indian tribes adapt their dwellings to the environment?"

ELLIOT: Should we read about every Indian tribe?

NANCY: Each one of us could take a different tribe . . .

BOB: But there are so many, and they live in such different places.

JEAN: We don't have to read about every tribe. Let's take those who live in totally different surroundings.

SHEL: I'd like to know why the ancient Indians lived the way they did.

ELLIOT: Well, should we stick to the tribes of today or study the ancient tribes, too?

JEAN: We have a lot of material on the Navajo . . .

After a while this group decided to study two tribes in particular and ancient Indian dwellings in general. They based their decision on their respective interests as well as on the resources available to them.

One group member will serve as recorder and write down everyone's questions. The first time a class undertakes Group Investigation the procedure at this stage may be somewhat schematic. If there are four students in the group, there may be eight questions, which they then divide among themselves. As the class becomes more comfortable with the process, it is not unusual for the group to start off with one idea and end up with quite another. The discussion at this stage will highlight group members' varying (and sometimes conflicting) points of view. In order to formulate their problem and determine their procedures, they have to reach an agreement that reconciles their differences.

The cooperative planning at this stage also enables each student to choose the type of investigation that best suits him or her. One student may prefer to read, another may enjoy interviewing people. Some students may feel they learn best when they build something or draw a diagram. For others it may be necessary to see for themselves the actual context of the problem, so they will prefer an "on-site" visit. Groups take into account their members' varied tendencies and preferences when they divide the parts of the investigation among themselves.

Many teachers find it useful to have groups fill out a worksheet that structures the steps of this planning stage, as shown in Figure 4.2.

A copy of each group's worksheet should be posted. In addition to serving as a reminder of what each group is doing, this display shows the connection between all the groups in the class. Each individual student contributes to the small group's investigation, and each group contributes to the whole class's study of the larger topic. The group cited in the worksheet, for example, was part of an eighth-

Figure 4.2   Group Planning Form

OUR RESEARCH TOPIC:	How did Indian tribes adapt their dwellings to their environment?
GROUP MEMBERS:	Bob, Elliot, Jean, Shel, and Nancy
ROLES:	Bob--coordinator; Jean and Nancy--resource persons; Elliot--steering committee; Shel--recorder
WHAT DO WE WANT TO FIND OUT?	Bob and Nancy--How did the nomadic Apaches design their shelters? Elliot and Jean--In what way did the hogans suit the Navajo way of life? Shel--What kind of dwellings did ancient Indians live in?
WHAT ARE OUR RESOURCES?	Under this heading the recorder will list the books to be read, the people to be interviewed, and the sites to be visited. Perhaps all five members of this group will visit the same site, but each one will prepare different questions to ask.

grade class in Arizona investigating the connection between homes and the environment. Other groups' subtopics were: (1) "In what ways are modern homes adapted to their environment?" (2) "How do modern cities affect the environment?" (3) "How will homes of the future be adapted to the environment?"

Teacher's Role.   As the teacher circulates among the groups, he or she offers help to those who need it. Perhaps one group is unhappy with their original plan. Instead of insisting that the group stick to a plan that has proven uninteresting to them, the teacher can discuss alternatives and help them redirect their goal. Another group may have planned to tackle too many questions. Again, the teacher can help them formulate more realistic plans.

The teacher also offers help in choosing appropriate resources. Perhaps the teacher knows someone who can meet with a group and provide information or guidance not available in books. Or maybe the teacher will point out a particular book or article that group members overlooked.

Some groups will need more direct help than others. One group may have a member who is particularly hesitant about expressing his or her interests. In order to draw the student out, the teacher may sit with him or her for a few minutes and offer reassurance and encouragement. By contrast, some groups may only need an occasional reminder that "If that's what interests you, by all means go ahead and investigate it." At all times the teacher should encourage students to plan diverse ways of investigating their subtopics.

Circulating from group to group gives the teacher a chance to see if any groups are having difficulty cooperating. Students may not be able to reach agreement on the scope of the investigation. Or perhaps one or two group members are not participating in the discussion. In such cases, the teacher has to intervene. As Cohen (1986) suggests, there are several ways to help the students without actually telling them what to do:

- Ask key questions to stimulate or redirect their thinking.
- Talk over how they are doing on some of the cooperative norms.
- Support and reinforce their efforts at solving their own problems.
- Ask a group to take a break from their work and spend 10 or 15 minutes on an exercise that will strengthen their ability to interact successfully.

Students' Roles.   Students plan their work cooperatively. They identify those aspects of their subtopic that they want to investigate and then plan how to proceed. They choose their resources and decide how to divide the assignments among themselves.

All the while they discuss with one another what they consider worth investigating, where they can get information, and how to go about it. They talk to one another, listen to one another, seek connections among their respective ideas and interests, and bear in mind what each one can contribute to the group's common plan.

Generally groups find it helpful to have one member serve as resource person and another as secretary or recorder in order to organize their work. The resource person coordinates the search for appropriate material. The recorder reminds group members what their roles are and what the deadline is for reporting back to the group. The recorder may also keep a record of everyone's progress.

The coordinator (or chairperson) serves as leader during group discussions when information is shared and plans are made. In addition, the coordinator encourages everyone to participate and contribute to the group's effort.

The students also choose one member to represent them in the classwide steering committee. Toward the end of stage IV this committee will hold several meetings with the teacher to coordinate the groups' presentations to the class.

Stage III: Groups Carry Out Their Investigations

At this stage each group carries out the plans decided upon in stage II. They locate the information they require, organize it, and interpret and integrate their findings. This is the longest stage and may span three or four class periods, if not more. Each class period at this stage begins with the teacher reviewing what each group plans to do that day. One or two group members may spend some time in the library, others may summarize their visit to a museum, while a few may interview a resource person inside the school. One group may view a filmstrip and read an article relevant to their investigation.

Locating Information.   Group members locate the information they require from a number of different sources: textbooks, encyclopedias, pamphlets, maps, biographies, and so forth. Some of these may be available in the classroom as well as in the school library; others may be available from public libraries or even students' homes. Another source of information may be a museum, a historical building, a national park, or any other site connected with the general problem. The list of sources of information can be expanded to include magazines, newspapers, stamps, films and videotapes, and, of course, other people, such as teachers, parents, or experts in the field.

The questions that the students asked about their specific subtopic guide them as they locate information. As they do in any situation that calls for locating information, students record the information they find: They make notes while they read, photocopy a few relevant pages, or tape the interview.

Organizing and Interpreting Information.   The next step in the investigation is to organize the information in any one of a number of ways, such as writing an outline or a short summary or drawing a graph, a diagram, or a chart. If information was gathered from more than one source, now is the time to analyze it and evaluate its relevance to the question or questions under investigation. Students also determine whether they have located sufficient information or whether there is need for more. Perhaps different sources present what seems like contradictory information or opinions. The students can turn to one another or to the teacher for clarification.

Whether students investigate a particular aspect of the group subtopic alone or with a partner, they will benefit from discussing their findings with other group members. At the beginning or end of every lesson at this stage, groups can meet to check their work in progress. Together they try to make sense out of all the material they have gathered, as did one group of fifth-graders while investigating the problem "How do we get energy from the sun?" Two group members, Lisa and Jeremy, began by reporting what they had read about the topic:

LISA: We read that the sun is on fire. The sun has millions of degrees of heat at its core that heats up the hydrogen gas atoms.

CAROLE: Where are the hydrogen gas atoms?

LISA: Oh, I didn't say it right. The sun is made up of hydrogen gas atoms, and the tremendous heat at the sun's core stirs them up. I can just see the atoms crashing into each other!

JEREMY: They crash into each other and explode. Imagine! Four million tons of hydrogen are turned into energy every second! Other parts shoot off into space like sprays of little bullets. That's the sunlight we get.

BERT: No wonder I got a sunburn last summer!
SHARON: And isn't hydrogen dangerous? Like a hydrogen
             bomb? Isn't the sun dangerous? We all know how
             we're supposed to be careful and put on globs of
             sunblock . . .
BERT: Tomorrow Carole and I are going to interview the
             science teacher about the benefits of the sun's
             energy. We could also ask her about the dangers of
             the sun's energy.

When Carole and Bert returned from their meeting with the science teacher, they read their summary to their groupmates. Sharon remarked that the facts were interesting, but the summary sounded too choppy. Jeremy noted that some of the information was similar to what he had read and added a few points to the report. They called the teacher over and asked her if she thought it was a good idea to include a paragraph on the sun's dangers in their final written report. The teacher pointed out that considering how the sun could be dangerous was an interesting part of their inquiry and would probably lead to a classwide discussion of how to protect ourselves from the sun. She felt that this issue was relevant to the class's general problem, "How on Earth are we related to the Sun and its family?"

Integrating Findings.   As their investigation draws to a close, the recorder notes the group's conclusions. Groups carrying out their first investigation, especially in the lower grades, may simply record each member's answer or a short summary of the question that he or she investigated.

Whereas at first the summary may be an accumulation of findings, after several Group Investigation projects it becomes an integration of findings. Students continue to share information, but they also go on to compare their respective findings and search for ways to apply them to their research problem. They weigh each contribution in terms of the light it sheds on the problem they set out to investigate. At this point students will often discover a new problem that evolves from the discussion of their findings, as did those students who investigated how the sun produces energy:

SHARON: (*chairperson*) Well, we've written about how we get
             energy from the sun and how we benefit from that
             energy and we have a list of dangers, too.

LISA: We also have a diagram of the different parts of the sun.

SHARON: Who has something else about energy from the sun?

BERT: Well, not all the energy comes directly from the sun.

LISA: How's that?

BERT: We get energy from coal and oil, and they got it from the sun long ago.

CAROLE: The science teacher told us that coal comes from masses of fallen plants that built up over time. And oil comes from the remains of billions and billions of tiny prehistoric water plants.

LISA: Won't we ever use up all that energy from the sun?

BERT: Is that possible?

JEREMY: That's why they're developing atomic energy! We could compare atomic energy to the sun's energy.

BERT: I don't think we should—that'll get us involved in all the dangers of atomic energy . . .

SHARON: Well, we could just mention at the end of our report that there are other sources of energy in addition to the sun . . . who would like to write about that?

Teacher's Role.   The teacher continues to support the groups in their efforts and provides help when needed. The help needed at this stage centers around study skills. While the students are searching for information and answers to their questions, the teacher checks to see if they make full use of the printed information at their disposal. Do students know how to use an index? Are all the terms in a particular source understood? Do the students make use of the table of contents? Can the students select the appropriate meanings of words in the dictionary?

In addition, students may need help utilizing other sources. Are the questions they prepared for an interview appropriate? Did they focus on the main idea of a documentary they watched? Do they need help recording the results of their experiment? Generally, different students need different degrees and kinds of help, but sometimes the teacher may discover that most or even all of the class is having a common difficulty. In that case, it is advisable to convene the whole class and review the problematic skill.

In some cases the teacher may decide that the whole class should acquire some specific information, despite the differences in the groups' subtopics. She may then ask each group to include a particular chapter or article in its list of sources. Or she may prepare a learning station and have all the groups work there in turns. If the investigation project is a particularly long one, the teacher may wish to reconvene the whole class after a few lessons and ask each group to report on its progress.

Students' Roles.   In this stage students are investigators: They turn to a variety of sources for answers to their questions, then they organize the information they have gathered and summarize it. They actually engage in problem solving instead of learning about problem solving.

Group members constantly coordinate their efforts in order to carry out their common goal. Each student becomes the group's "specialist" on a particular aspect of the group's subtopic. Each "specialist" contributes his or her knowledge to the group. Students interpret their findings individually as well as by discussing them with partners and with the whole group. At all times their work requires that they help one another and respect one another's interests. Finally, the group prepares a report that integrates the answers they found to the questions they set out to investigate together.

Stage IV: Groups Plan Their Presentations

At this stage groups decide which of their findings they will share with the class and how to present them. The group's presentation is not intended to teach their classmates everything they learned during their investigation. The central purpose of the presentation is to show the class what the group considers to be the main idea of their inquiry. In order to do so, they pull together all the parts of their investigation into an integrated whole and plan a presentation that will be both instructive and appealing to the rest of the class.

Identifying the Main Idea.   The first step in planning the presentation requires groups to determine the main idea of their findings. In their search for answers to their questions, they encountered a great deal of information from different sources. What do they feel is the most important aspect of the answers they came up with? The group studying the sources of the sun's energy, for instance, had to weigh several findings. They learned how the sun produces energy, they learned the benefits and dangers of this energy, and they became aware of other sources of energy. Now they must ask themselves new questions: Of all these answers, which is the most significant? Which will interest the class most and which is most related to the subtopics investigated by other groups? The teacher, who has been constantly observing the groups at work, will know which groups need help in deciding which is the main outcome of their investigation. The teacher's guidance helped the group that was investigating how the sun produces energy:

TEACHER: How are you doing with your plans for a presentation? What did you decide to emphasize?

CAROLE: Well, we have a diagram of the sun . . .

LISA: We could tell the class how the sun burns hydrogen and turns it into energy.

TEACHER: The class will want to know about that. What else?

SHARON: We learned about the benefits of the sun's energy and also about the dangers of the sun. Which is more important?

TEACHER: They're both important. What do you think?

The group struggled with that question for a while and finally decided that they would like to stress how our lives depend on energy from the sun. The teacher reminded them that they had a lot of material on how dangerous the sun could be and suggested that they include it in their presentation.

Presenting the Main Idea. In the second step of planning the presentation, group members decide how they will present their main findings. Many options are open for the way presentations can be made. These can be in the form of an exhibit, a model, a learning center, a written report, a dramatic presentation, a guided tour, or a slide presentation, to mention just a few. In addition to the presentation, groups prepare a handout that lists their resources and the most salient information they have gathered. This is an easy way of sharing basic facts and references. Since all groups investigated subtopics related in some way to a common general topic, there may be some overlapping in the list of resources or even in some of the basic data.

The following suggestions serve as guidelines to help groups plan their presentations:

- Emphasize the main ideas and conclusions of the investigation.
- Make sure everyone in the presenting group takes an active part in the presentation.
- Inform the class about the sources the group consulted in

order to get information. (The group may hand out a list of sources.)
- Set and observe time limits for the length of the presentations.
- Allow time for the rest of the class to ask questions.
- Involve classmates as much as possible in the presentation by giving them roles to perform.
- Make sure all required equipment and materials are available.

Most groups decide what their presentation will be after they have located, organized, and integrated all their information. Students in a group inquiring into the life of an author waited until all their data were collected in order to prepare a short skit on the most productive period of her life. The students who had investigated how the sun produces energy decided to do the following:

Lisa prepared a short explanation of how the sun produces energy. Together, all group members prepared a large mural depicting the sun and around it an array of plants, animals, and people. They added the title "What We Owe the Sun." Each member of the group prepared a paragraph explaining the connection between one of the items on the mural and the sun's energy. In addition they wrote a list of ways people can protect themselves from the sun, which they planned to hand out to the class.

For some groups the presentation begins to take shape while they are involved in their investigation. In the course of their inquiry, the group studying "What does it take to be an astronaut?" collected pictures, posters, and even stamps depicting several astronauts and scientists. They decided to use this material as the basis for a learning center, that they presented to the class.

Teacher's Role.   At this stage of the class's investigation, the teacher organizes and coordinates the groups' plans for their presentations. When the teacher notes that the groups are nearing the end of their investigations, it is time to convene the members of the steering committee (who were chosen in stage II). The committee hears each group's plan for its report. The teacher writes down each group's requests for special materials and coordinates the time schedule. With the teacher's guidance, the committee members make sure that the ideas for presentation are varied and clear and can indeed be carried out. The teacher continues in the role of advisor, helps the committee where needed, and reminds them that each group's plan should involve all its members.

Students' Roles. During the planning discussions that the groups conduct at this stage, they assume a new role—that of "teacher." True, group members have been telling one another all along about their work and continually discussing what they did or did not understand. In that sense they have been tutoring one another every step of the way. But now they begin to plan how to teach their classmates, in a more organized way, the essence of what they have learned. As they plan their presentations, they continue to talk and listen to one another, to exchange ideas and information, and to plan their actions cooperatively.

Stage V: Groups Make Their Presentations

The groups are now prepared to present their findings to the class. The class is reconvened so that each group can shed its specific light on the class's common concern. The schedule of presentations decided upon by the teacher and the steering committee is posted so that each group knows when its turn will come. It usually requires two class periods to complete this stage.

While one group makes its presentation, the rest are a receptive "audience." The audience knows enough about the problem to enable it to understand the presentation, yet they will hear and see the problem approached from several different angles. Each member of the audience can see what other groups add to his or her understanding of the general topic.

It helps to have each student fill out a short questionnaire during the presentation. The teacher and the students should decide together which questions are most appropriate. These questions may refer to the content of the presentation as well as to the way it was organized. The following are a few suggestions:

What was the main idea of the presentation?
Did each group member participate?
Do you feel the group used its resources well?
What did you like best about the presentation?

After each presentation a few minutes are set aside for the audience's comments. This is a good opportunity to conduct a whole-class discussion on the relationship between all the presentations.

An example of the diversity of reports that groups can present comes from a sixth-grade class in Tel Aviv that investigated the legacy of ancient Greece. One group, which had investigated the legacy of democracy, began its presentation by explaining how Athens was governed. Afterwards, they informed the class that they were going to conduct a trial. They were all "citizens" of Athens and judges were to be selected from among them, as in ancient times. The "case" brought before the "court" concerned a teacher who did not conduct her class democratically. Judges were selected by lots and came to the front of the room, where the accused and witnesses for both sides sat. After hearing the pleas for the defense and the prosecution, the judges put their tallies in a box. When the tallies were removed, it turned out that the "teacher" was found guilty—not to anyone's great surprise.

In the same class another group, which had investigated ancient Greek mythology, read aloud the story of Pandora's box and prepared a quiz show about the Olympic gods. The group made figurines of the best-known Greek gods. Each group member had a turn presenting a figurine and asking the members of the class to identify the god and tell something about it. A third group studied about art and architecture in ancient Greece. They gave short talks about each of the arts in ancient Greece and then displayed a large model of the Parthenon that they had built. They explained the structure and functions of temples and then invited the class to ask any questions they had about temples in ancient Greece.

Another group's presentation included a dictionary of words in modern Hebrew that have Greek roots and a learning center where students were asked to write sentences using these words. The learning center remained in the class for two weeks and students worked there individually. The group that investigated theater dramatized the battle of Achilles and Hector at the walls of Troy. The most fun of all was the presentation of the group that had studied sports in ancient Greece. They organized a miniature series of Olympic games that took the whole class outside for half a day.

Fortunately, we were able to observe the teacher and the students in this class for two years, as they changed from a very traditional fifth grade to a fully cooperative sixth grade. To be sure, their first attempts at Group Investigation did not result in presentations as spectacular as the ones described above. The students were hesitant and even wary about making choices independently of the teacher with respect to other aspects of the investigation as well (S. Sharan & Hertz-Lazarowitz, 1980). After several Group Investigation projects, the students in this class were able to plan their work effectively and were especially inventive in planning their presentations.

Teacher's Role.   At this stage the teacher serves as coordinator of the groups' presentations. He or she also becomes a member of the audience. It is the teacher's turn to sit back and enjoy the way each group communicates what it considers to be the essence of its work.

At the end of each presentation, the teacher leads a short discussion of the audience's comments on what they saw. These comments are based on their answers to the four or five questions agreed upon by the whole class. The various answers supply the presenters with instant reactions to their efforts. They also indicate to what extent the students connect their own subtopics with what they hear and see. For example, when the children in the above-mentioned sixth grade asked questions about the Greek temples or identified the gods and their functions, they were relating what they had learned in their own inquiries to other aspects of the common problem studied by the class.

Standing before an audience and speaking may cause some students to be hesitant and self-conscious. They now have to take into account the needs of a larger group, which requires a more organized presentation of ideas than did small-group discussions. Although the teacher helped the groups prepare their presentations, some students may still be uncomfortable at this stage. It is necessary, therefore, to make sure that students in the audience express their reactions but do not become unduly critical. Rules for conducting the short discussion after each presentation should be established beforehand.

Students' Roles.   The students have diverse roles in this stage. First and foremost, they are presenters. They present their most significant findings to their classmates in an organized fashion and in the most attractive way possible. They are also resource persons, sharing their resources with fellow investigators.

Throughout this stage they represent the small group that investigated a particular subtopic. At the same time they are members of the large group that investigated a common general problem. They present the one aspect of the general problem they know best and simultaneously become aware of other facets of the same problem.

Students reflect on the clarity, appeal, and relevance of other students' presentations. This is their opportunity to observe how other groups organized their findings and thus add to their own repertoire of ways and means of making presentations. Finally, as members of a cooperative classroom, students are responsible for expressing their comments as constructively as they can.

The presentations are a culminating activity as well as a beginning. They demonstrate that each group has earned its position as a potential resource for others who may, in the future, wish to learn more about its specific area of investigation (Thelen, 1981). The impressions the teacher gathers from the students' reactions to all the presentations are part of the evaluation process, which is the final stage of the project.

Stage VI: Teacher and Students Evaluate Their Projects

Evaluation focuses on the knowledge acquired in the course of the investigation as well as on the experience of investigating. Both these aspects of evaluation may be conducted on an individual, group, and class basis.

Collaborative Evaluation.   Comments by the class after each presentation are one example of classwide assessment, where the teacher and students collaborate in order to evaluate the outcome of the investigation.

Students and teachers can also collaborate in the construction of a test made up of questions that the groups submit, based on the main ideas of their findings, which they determined in stage IV. In a class of seven groups, for example, each group suggests 2 questions. The test would then consist of 14 questions. Each student answers 12 questions, excluding those submitted by his or her group. This is how the teacher of the sixth-grade class that investigated the legacy of ancient Greece chose to evaluate the class's learning. She handed out the list of questions to all the students and allotted them a week for preparation. She suggested that in addition to consulting their textbook and other printed material, the children ask their classmates for information and clarification. This was yet another opportunity for the children to share their respective expertise with their classmates.

After the test, the teacher asked each group to discuss how it understood the connection between its specific subtopic and the other subtopics. How did democracy in ancient Greece influence architecture, sports, language, and so forth? Conversely, how was the ancient Greek language a mirror for democracy, sports, mythology, theater, and so forth? After the group discussions, the teacher led the class in a final wrap-up of what they had all learned about the legacy of ancient Greece.

Evaluating Factual Knowledge.   It is safe to assume that in the course of the investigation students learn many new facts. If the teacher wishes to assess this kind of learning, the test should include questions that require students to recall details that they encountered in the various sources they consulted during the investigation.

The investigation also exposes students to new terms. Questions in this category might require students to define terms or to compare terms. For example, in order to see how well the students understood the terms related to the sun's energy, they were asked two questions:

Explain what happens when sunlight hits the atmosphere.
Describe the effect sunspots have on our planet.

Another way of testing the students' knowledge of facts and terms that are germaine to the Group Investigation project is to present them as part of a learning center, as we suggested in stage III. Activity cards at the center, at which students work individually or in pairs, can focus on the detailed, factual knowledge that the teacher would like everyone to learn.

The teacher also evaluates how each student *integrated* all the information he or she acquired in the course of the investigation. One way of assessing this is to pose questions that ask them to explain what causes a particular phenomenon or event, such as "How do sun, air, and water make weather?" or "What do you think are the most important traits of an astronaut?"

Ongoing Evaluation.   Less structured ways of evaluating outcomes as well as the process of investigation are employed throughout the first five stages. Students are constantly discussing their work among themselves and with the teacher, thus making their grasp of their topic highly visible at all times. As he or she goes from group to group, the teacher has ample opportunities to form reliable judgments about the goals the students have set for themselves and the ways they have chosen to reach them. The teacher can gauge the extent to which the students are clarifying the subtopics they undertook to investigate and judge the degree to which they are benefiting from the various sources at their disposal.

The ease with which children *cooperate* in the course of the investigation is also highly visible to the teacher. Circulating among the groups, the teacher can see how well discussions are conducted, whether everyone indeed participates, and whether there are any factors that stand in the way of the group's working together efficiently.

The ongoing evaluation that takes place throughout the course of the investigation is clearly diagnostic. It has the advantage of enabling the teacher to spot a snag in the process of investigation and intervene before it becomes a major obstacle. If a group does not seem able to make realistic plans or is having difficulty carrying out its plans, the teacher can help the students before their work is seriously disrupted (see the suggestions on p. 79).

Reflective Evaluation. As they circulate among the groups to see what they can learn about their students' academic and social behavior, teachers can also ask the students what they feel about their learning. One way of initiating such a discussion is to ask how the students feel about the content of the investigation:

What material was most interesting to you?
How do you feel about the conclusions in this chapter?
Did you learn anything that surprises you?

Other questions may deal with the way the group is functioning:

Is everyone taking part?
Are you having any difficulties in working together?
In what way are you working better than you did in the last investigation project?

Questions like these, asked of individuals as well as of groups, are based on the norm of reflection that is an integral part of cooperative learning. By drawing the students out, the teacher helps them articulate the meaning that the cooperative investigation has for each one of them. They come to understand that the substance of their learning includes the personal meaning it has for them. Students cannot be *taught* what meaning their learning has for them, and obviously they cannot be graded on it. However, they can be coached to pay attention to what they think and how they feel about what and how they learn. By doing so the teacher establishes this type of personal evaluation as a valued element of the learning process.

Evaluating Higher-Level Thinking.   Assessment of learning in Group Investigation should evaluate students' higher-level thinking about the topics they studied. They should be asked to demonstrate their ability to draw conclusions and to apply their new knowledge to new problems and situations.

Much of the evidence about students' application of higher-level thinking skills is gathered during the ongoing evaluation. Every time the teacher meets with an individual student or with a group, the discussion reveals which thinking skills are in use and how effectively they are being used. The questions students ask as well as the way each group organizes its findings, determines the main ideas of its findings, prepares its presentation, and discovers the relationship among all subtopics are further evidence of thinking skills that go beyond learning and recalling new facts and terms. However, there is room for more deliberate evaluation of the higher-level thinking skills involved in the investigation. Specific questions that tap these skills may be included in a test that the teacher constructs, and they may also be evaluated by *special assignments.*

One example of such an assignment comes from the class that investigated the general problem "How on Earth are we related to the Sun and its family?" as part of the unit on the solar system. As part of the evaluation, the teacher suggested that the class put out a newspaper called *Solar News.* Each group chose one member to represent them on the editorial board, which then met together with the teacher to suggest what kind of material each group would prepare. Among the items in the paper was a travel column based on an imaginary visit to "Our Neighbor—The Moon"; there were several advertisements for different devices, real and imaginary, for saving solar energy; one article was based on various legends and myths about the sun; and, of course, there was a health column instructing readers how to protect themselves from the sun's rays. Evaluation of all the material submitted for "publication" was undertaken jointly by the teacher and the editorial board.

A different assignment was given to the class that investigated the importance of space exploration. There the teacher combined individual and group evaluation of higher-level thinking. At first she asked each student to pretend to be a retired astronaut and write a letter to a grandchild about the most exciting event in his or her work. The evaluation was based on the extent to which the description of the event included details of the life and work of an astronaut and an understanding of the problems he or she faces.

Afterwards, each group was asked to discuss and then write a summary of what they thought space exploration had achieved, what they saw as new frontiers for space exploration, and in what ways it might help humanity. This summary reflected what they had learned as a class as well as how they evaluated the significance of what they had learned.

Teacher's Role.   In actual practice, the teacher's role as evaluator does not begin at the last stage. Throughout the investigation he or she is in a unique position to evaluate what the students are learning, how they are getting along in their groups, and what the specific strengths and weaknesses of individuals are. Formative evaluation takes place at each stage.

Since teachers have many opportunities to observe their students' activities and performance, it is helpful to record these observations on a checklist. The items on the checklist should be suited to the many learning goals of the investigation project and should enable the teacher to note how the students are developing as investigators. Several questions on the checklist should refer to reflective evaluation, as we noted above. It should also include items that tap students' ability to engage in cooperative planning, locate and organize information from a variety of sources, summarize and integrate their findings, and use different modes of thought (analyze, evaluate, create imaginary applications of the information obtained during the investigation). These goals are also assessed by more structured and formal means, as we suggested in the beginning of this section.

Although students are not graded at every stage of the investigation, they do not have to wait until after they have finished in order to find out how well they are doing or what problems they have. Once the groups begin their work, the teacher does not leave them on their own. He or she is always there to acknowledge the students' efforts, encourage them to seek answers to their questions, and help them when necessary. In this way the teacher also helps maintain students' incentive to carry out their plans. This is especially important for students who are new to Group Investigation. The teacher will have to clearly specify the criteria for evaluation and the means by which he or she chooses to carry it out. Most teachers prefer to combine individual testing for a grade with a verbal evaluation of the group's product in one of the several ways described above.

Students' Roles.   In the evaluation stage students have the opportunity to refine their awareness of their performance as investigators and as group members. If, for instance, they are asked to contrib-

Table 4.1 Stages of Group Investigation, Teacher's Roles and Students' Roles

STAGE OF GROUP INVESTIGATION	TEACHER'S ROLE	STUDENTS' ROLE
I. Class determines sub-topics and organizes into research groups	Leader of exploratory discussions that determine subtopics; facilitator of awareness of interesting aspects of general topic	Generate questions of interest; sort them into categories; join research group of choice
II. Groups plan their investigation: what they will study and how they will go about it	Helps groups formulate their plans; helps maintain cooperative group norms; helps find source materials	Plan what to study; choose resources; assign roles and divide the study task among themselves
III. Groups carry out the investigation	Helps with study skills; continues to help maintain cooperative group norms	Seek answers to their questions; locate information from a variety of sources; integrate and summarize their findings
IV. Groups plan their presentations	Organizes plans for presentations and coordinates them with the steering committee	Determine main idea of their findings; plan how to transmit it to the class
V. Groups make their presentations	Coordinates presentations; conducts discussions of feedback	Presenters; give feedback to classmates about their presentations
VI. Teacher and students evaluate Group Investigation individually, in groups, and classwide	Evaluates learning of new information, higher level thinking, and cooperative behavior	Refine awareness of performance as investigators and as group members

ute questions to a classwide examination, they have to think about the most meaningful aspects of their inquiry as well as about what might interest their classmates. Their awareness is further enhanced during the short but frequent evaluative talks with the teacher. As they answer the teacher's questions, they increase their ability to reflect on the way they carry out their investigation and on the way they cooperate with their peers.

The students' central role throughout the investigation is to actively make sense of their learning. They do this when they

- Ask questions pertinent to the subject and to their personal interests
- Cooperate with their teammates in the search for answers
- Contribute their thoughts, ideas, and knowledge to the group effort
- Make use of their peers' contributions
- Increase their competence in all these areas

Table 4.1 (preceding page) summarizes the stages of Group Investigation as well as the teacher's and students' roles in each stage.

Group Investigation provides the setting for learning that combines personal, social, and academic meaning. Teachers and students help one another nurture the emotional involvement and the mental stimulation that make Group Investigation an authentic experience.

5

Examples of Group Investigation Projects

with DINA SHEMER

The stages of Group Investigation serve as a general outline for the implementation of cooperative planning and learning. They are not meant to be replicated in the same way time and again. The stages are helpful because they provide teachers and students with a set of guidelines, yet allow for a great deal of choice and flexibility. In order to illustrate how this can be done, we present four examples of the application of Group Investigation in different subjects and grade levels:

- What and how do animals eat? (grade 3 science class)
- How did explorers change the world? (grade 6 geography class)
- What makes a poem a poem? (grade 10 English class)
- What do stamps teach us about the United States? (grade 4)

Finally, we present an example of how Group Investigation was employed by a high school as part of an effort to deal with a community problem and to strengthen the ties between the community and the school.

WHAT AND HOW DO ANIMALS EAT?
A Third-Grade Group Investigation Project

Ms. Jacobs's third-grade class was studying about animals. She planned to devote several lessons to the study of animals' eating habits and chose Group Investigation as the method of study. Although the science textbook described several animals in each of the five classes of vertebrates, Ms. Jacobs felt that Group Investigation would enable the children to learn from a wider range of sources and become more directly involved in planning what to study.

Ms. Jacobs planned to launch the investigation project with a visit to the local zoo. In preparation, she called the youth department at the zoo and arranged for one of the guides to conduct a tour at the time the animals were being fed. She learned that they were also prepared to show the children a short film on desert animals that demonstrated how they get their food and how the design of their bodies helps them survive in the desert.

She also approached the eighth-grade science teacher, who agreed to host a few children in the lab, where there was a small collection of frogs and toads. In addition, Ms. Jacobs found appropriate information in some science magazines and in two encyclopedias from the school library. Although not all the material was at the appropriate grade level, Ms. Jacobs was prepared to devote time to assisting those children who might need help.

On one of the walls in the classroom Ms. Jacobs prepared a display area. She hung up a large piece of oaktag with the title "What Do We Want to Find Out About Animals' Eating Habits?"

Stage I: Class Determines Subtopics and Organizes into Research Groups

Presenting the General Problem. Ms. Jacobs told the class that they would be studying animals' eating habits and would begin by visiting the zoo. "You've all been to the zoo, I'm sure, but this time I'm going to ask you to concentrate on finding out what the animals eat. We're going to go at feeding time and meet with the keepers who feed the animals. Afterwards, one of the guides will meet with us. What would you like to ask him?"

Most of the children were very enthusiastic, although a few had their doubts about what they might learn:

SCOTT: We could ask about all the different kinds of food they eat . . .

NINA: Yeah, but the zookeeper gives them food so we can't see how they get their food, like in the jungle . . .

PETER: We could see different animals, I mean not just the ones we read about.

MIKEY: But maybe they won't want to eat when we're there.
HAN: So, we could ask the people who take care of them
          . . .
BILLY: Maybe we'll see how snakes stretch their mouths!
HILARY: How come they can open their mouths so wide!
JO: I want to know if fish have teeth and if they chew.
ROSA: Do they swallow water when they swallow the fish
          they eat?

The list of questions kept growing. Finally, Ms. Jacobs pointed out that they could all be summarized by two main questions, which she wrote on the poster hanging in the display area:

1. What kinds of food do the animals in each class eat?
2. How do the animals eat their food?

Before the trip each child received a chart of the five classes of vertebrates and the type of food they might eat (see Figure 5.1). Ms. Jacobs asked the children to pair off during the trip and try to fill in as many names as possible.

The following day the class set out for the zoo. They saw most of the animals during feeding time and watched intently. They went from one area to another, listened to the guide's explanations, and filled out their charts. At the end of their tour, the guide showed them the film on how desert animals find food. The children had never been to the desert and were fascinated by what they saw. The guide

Figure 5.1   What Do Animals Eat?

	Who Eats Plants?	Who Eats Meat?	Who Eats Both?
Amphibians			
Fish			
Reptiles			
Birds			
Mammals			

also answered many of their questions about what and how the animals eat.

Back in the classroom the next day, Ms. Jacobs suggested that the children write their impressions of their visit. Some children wrote poems, others described the visit, and a few wrote about the work of a zookeeper.

Determining Questions for Group Inquiry.
At the next lesson, Ms. Jacobs introduced the cooperative planning of questions for investigation. She asked the children if the trip to the zoo supplied the answers to the two questions they set out to answer. They all had something to say. Some of their comments were:

DON:	We saw the tiger eating a real hunk of meat.
NINA:	The eagle also had meat.
HAN:	The owls were eating chicken wings.
MS. JACOBS:	Do all birds eat meat or chicken?
BILLY:	I saw them put seeds and fruit out for the cardinals.
KEN:	But that's not how they eat in the forest . . .
HILARY:	Or in the jungle . . . I still don't know how they always find food there.
PETER:	We only saw what they get in the zoo . . . what the keepers give them.
ROSA:	I forgot to ask the guide what happens to the fish when they swallow all that water. How come they don't burst? Too bad the movie was only about the desert . . .
SHARON:	I didn't know that there were so many animals in the desert.
SUE:	. . . and the movie showed us how the design of the snake's body helps it get food in the desert.
PETER:	Like the eagle's beak . . .
TOMMY:	And the giraffe's long neck . . .

Ms. Jacobs summed up the visit to the zoo by saying, "You've all learned what different animals eat. You saw that not all birds eat the same kind of food. Not all mammals eat the same kind of food. . . . In each class of animals not all the animals eat the same kind of food. I see you have more questions about how animals eat. Let me add them to our list." She wrote:

3. How do animals get their food out in the wild?
4. How are the animals' bodies and mouths built to help them get their food?

The next step was to introduce the Group Investigation project.

Forming Interest Groups. Ms. Jacobs wrote each of the five classes of vertebrates on the board. These served as the subtopics of the investigation project. She then had the children form groups. There were 35 children in the class, who would form seven groups with five members in each. The children numbered off from 1 to 7; all the 1's were in one group, all the 2's in another group, and so forth.

When the groups were formed, Ms. Jacobs asked each group to choose a class of animals. Two groups chose mammals, two groups chose birds, and one group each chose amphibians, fish, and reptiles.

Ms. Jacobs pointed out the table of books and magazines that she had prepared and asked that the students bring from home whatever additional books, pictures, slides, and even games that would help them learn about animals' eating habits.

Stage II: Groups Plan Their Investigations

The next day the children came into class with lots of material. They brought a variety of reference books; some brought old copies of *National Geographic* and other magazines, and a few brought some commercial games about animals. They placed all the material on two tables, together with the material that Ms. Jacobs had prepared. She told them that one by one each group would have a chance to look over the materials and choose what they needed.

Each group found a card on its table, on which Ms. Jacobs had printed instructions under the caption "Find Out What Mammals [Reptiles, Fish, etc.] Eat." There were three instructions:

1. Everyone in the group should choose one animal to study.
2. Choose a recorder who will write down everyone's name and the animal he or she chooses.
3. Look for information in our science textbook, in the books on the tables, and in photographs and slides.

The children began planning which animals they would study. As she went around the room, Ms. Jacobs heard the group that had chosen mammals dictating their choice of animal to their recorder. Mikey, a very shy child, could not seem to choose an animal. Ms. Jacobs tried to help him:

MS. JACOBS: Which mammal did you choose, Mikey?

MIKEY: I'm not sure . . .

MS. JACOBS: You mean you're not sure which animal you'd like to learn about?

MIKEY: No, I was wondering about whales, but I don't know if they're fish or mammals.

MS. JACOBS: Oh, I see. Well, whales are mammals. If you want to find out about whales tell Jose so that he'll write it down. What do you want to find out about them?

MIKEY: I know they . . . do they eat fish?

MS. JACOBS: Sure, but that's not all . . . and not all whales eat the same kind of food. Here, look in this book and see what you can find out.

Stage III: Groups Carry Out Their Investigations

Individual Study. For this stage Ms. Jacobs combined two periods so that the children could work uninterruptedly. They were to fill out individual worksheets that included the four questions the class had agreed upon as well as a question about resources (see Figure 5.2).

The class was a hub of activity. Everyone was busy looking up information about the animal he or she had chosen. Some were reading and others were looking at pictures. One group was looking at Neil's slides of his family's trip to the San Diego Zoo.

Ms. Jacobs approached the five children who had chosen amphibians. All five of them were interested in frogs and toads; none wanted to study any other amphibian. Since there was plenty of reading material for them, Ms. Jacobs accepted their plan. In addition, she told them that they could go up to the eighth-grade science lab. There the science teacher would meet with them and show them the frogs in the lab.

Andy, a member of the group studying reptiles, asked Ms. Jacobs for help. He was having trouble understanding the caption to a photograph in a magazine, which mentioned the snake's "specialized sort of feeding." Ms. Jacobs asked if any other member of the group could help and led them in a short discussion to clarify the difficulty.

Figure 5.2   What Do Animals Eat?

Write the name of the animal you chose: _____

1.   What kinds of food does it eat?

   _____

   _____

2.   How does it eat its food?

   _____

   _____

3.   How does it get its food?

   _____

   _____

4.   How are its body and mouth built to help it get its food?

   _____

   _____

5.   How did you find this out? Write down where you got your information.

   _____

   _____

   _____

Group Summary.   At the next session Ms. Jacobs told the class that each group would now put together what all its members had learned. She asked that the children read the first three answers on their worksheets to one another. Then she proposed that they compare their answers to the fourth question and write a summary titled "How reptiles' (fishes', amphibians', etc.) bodies are built to help them get their food." The recorder in each group wrote the group's summary on a separate piece of paper.

Ms. Jacobs went from group to group, helping them out when necessary. When she approached the group that had studied fish, she noted that their summary was quite limited: "Fish have pointed bodies so they can swim fast." She tried to help them expand this point.

MS. JACOBS:	That's true. But let's think—why do you think they have to swim fast?
DON:	They swim fast so they can catch other fish.
ROSA:	How come they don't swallow the water?
MS. JACOBS:	We'll get back to that question right away. First let's finish talking about why they swim so fast.
TOMMY:	I guess some fish swim fast so they can catch other fish and some fish swim fast so they can run away and not get eaten.
MS. JACOBS:	That's a good way of putting it. What do you think helps them swim fast, besides their pointed bodies?
DON:	Their fins . . .
TOMMY:	And their tails . . . they beat their tails and that makes them move.
PETER:	Like a propeller . . . and they're pointed in the front so they cut through the water.
MS. JACOBS:	You mentioned all the ways their bodies are designed to make it easy for them to swim and catch their food. Why not write all that down? While Don [the recorder] writes, think about Rosa's question—what happens to all the water that goes in their mouths?
SHARON:	The guide at the zoo said . . . he talked about that . . . how they have gills on the side of their mouths.
PETER:	He said that the water goes out through the gills. It's here in this book, too . . . look at this picture of the fish's mouth.
MS. JACOBS:	That's actually a diagram. See the gills on the side of the body, behind the mouth?
TOMMY:	If the water wouldn't go out, the fish would burst with all that water inside its mouth.
ROSA:	He said that the gills are like window slats, or like flaps . . . they don't let the food out, just the water.

MS. JACOBS: And the oxygen stays in, too. There's oxygen in the water, and the fish needs it to breath. The oxygen stays in, and the water goes out. Well, I think that now you can write how gills help the fish keep their food inside their bodies.

At the end of the allotted time, each group pasted their individual sheets onto one large sheet of paper, on which Ms. Jacobs had printed the question "What did you learn about the eating habits of fish [reptiles, mammals, etc.]?" In addition, each group's recorder hung the group's summary on the poster. The children decorated the posters with photographs, pictures, and drawings. A few children even brought stamps depicting animals and added them to the poster.

As the completed posters filled the wall, the children began reading one another's work. They were visibly impressed by this evidence of their investigations and asked that the posters remain on the wall a long time.

Stage IV: Groups Plan Their Presentations

Because the posters on the wall made all the group findings available to everyone, Ms. Jacobs did not think it necessary to have each group read its summary aloud to the rest of the class. Instead she suggested that each group choose one of two ways to present their findings to the class:

1. Prepare a television "documentary" about how the animals you studied find food in the wild. Draw the scenes of your documentary (or use photographs) and write the captions underneath.
2. Prepare a quiz for the class about how and what animals eat. The questions should be about all the animals we learned about.

Ms. Jacobs asked each group to choose one member to participate in the preparation of a game about animals' eating habits. The game would reflect every group's findings and would enable the class to review them and have fun at the same time.

Ms. Jacobs supplied those who chose to make a "television documentary" with a long roll of white paper. The children brought cardboard boxes for the TV "set." They attached both ends of the roll of paper to rolling pins so that they could show one scene at a time. The children in each group divided among themselves the tasks of drawing and writing.

The groups who chose to make up a quiz based their questions on the information posted on the wall. They divided the work among themselves, with each child in the group writing a few questions; the group then combined them all into one quiz.

Group representatives who took part in making the game received a large cardboard square and colored posterboard, scissors, and paste. The children brought pictures of all the animals they had learned about. The large board was divided into an equal number of squares, on which the children posted pictures of animals. They also prepared two sets of cards, one red and one blue, on which they wrote information about the animals' eating habits. The object of the game was to match the information on the card to the picture of the animal on the board. Whoever got a row of cards first was the winner.

All the individual worksheets were photocopied and placed in the box in which the game was kept. That way any time children were stuck for an answer they could look it up on the worksheets. Copies of worksheets for each of the five classes of animals were pasted on different colored paper so that they were easily distinguishable one from the other.

Stage V: Groups Make Their Presentations

The day on which the presentations took place had a festive air about it. A few parents contributed "people food," which was set out on a table at one end of the room. All the desks were lined up against the walls and the children placed their chairs in rows, as if in a theater. The four groups that had prepared "documentaries" alternated with the three groups that quizzed the class about what and how animals eat. After the last presentation, the group that had prepared the game explained it to the class.

Stage VI: Teacher and Students Evaluate Their Projects

The evaluation of this project included an individual assessment of what each child had learned as well as reflective assessment of how each group conducted its work and what they felt they had learned.

Individual Evaluation. Ms. Jacobs gave individual children written evaluations of their individual worksheets, based on how well they had used the available resources.

Reflective Evaluation of Group Investigation.   Since this was the first time her class had carried out a Group Investigation project, Ms. Jacobs wanted to give each group an opportunity to express their views and feelings about the experience. She met with each group separately and began the discussion by saying: "Think about all the ways you learned about what and how animals eat. We went to the zoo, saw a movie, and talked to the guide. You used a lot of different books and pictures. Which material did you like best? What was the most interesting? What are the most interesting things you learned?"

After hearing the students' reactions to these questions, Ms. Jacobs went on to ask about two other aspects of their work: (1) "How do you feel about working together in groups? What did you like about it? Did you have any difficulties working together?" (2) "When we carry out another Group Investigation project, what do you think we should do the same way we did this time? What do you think we should do differently?"

Peter summed up the success of the class's first attempt at Group Investigation when he said: "At first I thought—oh, no, not the zoo again, I've been there so many times. But I saw that there was a lot to learn and, anyway, this time I could ask about what I wanted to find out. And [in school] we didn't have to hurry . . . there was time to talk about things in the group . . ."

Many children suggested that next time there should be a vocabulary list to make it easier for them to understand the hard words they come across in their reading. Most of the children felt that the presentations were the best part of the project. A few said that they especially liked the way the teacher helped them in their groups. "It was easier to understand that way."

Ms. Jacobs planned to carry out another Group Investigation project the following month, on the social behavior of animals.

HOW DID EXPLORERS CHANGE THE WORLD?
A Sixth-Grade Group Investigation Project

When they studied about Columbus, Mr. Garrett's sixth-grade social studies class was very impressed by the explorer's courage and patience. The textbook's vivid descriptions made the children aware of the fact that Columbus knew where he wanted to go and, despite the dangers involved, had the persistence to get there. Their curiosity about explorers was aroused, and Mr. Garrett decided to expand the unit to include four other explorers from the Renaissance: Magellan, Vasco da Gama, Verrazano, and Hudson, as well as the famous Captain Cook.

There was not enough time to study about each explorer in depth, yet Mr. Garrett did not want the children to learn only the facts about where, when, and how each explorer ventured out into the world. He therefore chose to conduct a Group Investigation of the general problem "How did these explorers change the world?" He felt that by seeking answers to this problem the students would learn the basic facts about the explorers and deepen their appreciation of their enormous influence on the world.

Mr. Garrett planned to conduct the investigation in two parts. First, the class would break up into groups, with each group investigating the expeditions and discoveries of one explorer. Then they would regroup and share their expertise, "jigsaw" fashion (S. Sharan & Y. Sharan, 1976; Slavin, 1990). The new groups would tackle the question of how the five explorers' discoveries changed the world. Because the class was a relatively small one, with only 25 pupils, Mr. Garrett thought this was a very convenient way for groups to pool their information and attempt to address the general problem.

Because the textbook mentioned two of the five explorers very briefly, and the others not at all, Mr. Garrett found several books on the subject in the school library, including a variety of encyclopedias. He also looked for sources other than books. In the Acknowledgments section of one of the books he found the names of a nautical museum and a marine historical association. He wrote to them and asked for pictures and information about navigation and ships in the fifteenth and sixteenth centuries.

Terms such as *longitude* and *latitude* had been clarified during the study of Columbus's voyages. Now that his students would be reading about explorers more independently, Mr. Garrett anticipated that they might have difficulty understanding the various instruments used for maritime navigation. He therefore called the local chapter of the Boy Scouts and arranged for a scout master to come to the class and explain how compasses and other instruments work.

Stage I: Class Determines Subtopics and Organizes into Research Groups

Mr. Garrett introduced the investigation: "We learned how Columbus set out to find a new route to India. Before and after Columbus, other explorers also looked for new routes to the riches of India and China. They didn't always find what they were looking for, but they did find new lands, new products, and new people. All of them made their world a different place. Here are the names of five of the most famous explorers. Let's try to find out how each of them helped change the world they knew."

Cooperative Planning.   The names of the explorers were posted on the wall in a special display area. Mr. Garrett explained that the class would break up into groups, with each group investigating one explorer. Before they formed study groups, the class suggested questions for the investigation. Based on what they had learned about Columbus, the children had a good idea of what they wanted to know about other explorers.

The process began with pairs writing down what they wanted to find out. Ten minutes later two pairs compared their lists, adding and deleting questions as they talked. Ten minutes later each foursome read its questions to the class, and Mr. Garrett wrote them on the board. By the time the last foursome reported, there were few additions to be made. The final list consisted of eight questions:

1. Where did the explorer live?
2. What made him become an explorer?
3. What did he set out to discover?
4. How did he navigate?
5. What kinds of maps did he have?
6. Where did he get money for his ventures?
7. What were the hardships on the voyages?
8. What did he discover and what did he bring back to his country?

Study groups were formed on the basis of interest, one group for each explorer. All groups had five members.

Toward the end of the lesson, Mr. Garrett led the class in a discussion of where appropriate source materials could be found. He told them of the books he had located in the school library that they could use. The children named the books they had at home.

Stage II: Groups Plan Their Investigations

The list of questions was distributed to all the children and served as the basis for each group's investigation. All the source materials were placed on a table in the display area. The children in each group planned how to divide the questions and source materials among themselves. They listed the books they had at home and decided what they would read in class and what they would read at home. In each group one child was given the job of searching for material in the public library. Each group posted its plan in the display area under the name of the appropriate explorer. Each group chose a chairperson to coordinate the group's investigation.

Stage III: Groups Carry Out Their Investigations

One double period a week for two weeks was devoted to the investigation. Every aspect of the investigation was fascinating. At home and in school the children eagerly read accounts of the explorers' lives and adventures, the dangers they encountered, and their successes. The more difficult texts were scanned for their pictures. Because of the complexity of the topic, Mr. Garrett suggested that groups pool their information at the end of each session instead of waiting for the end of their search.

The first interim report already presented dramatic details about the various facets of the topic. In the group studying Magellan, for example, a group member was reading a short paragraph she had written about how the Spanish court sponsored him but gave him old ships and inferior crews. Another group member held the group spellbound as he described the "stinking water" the crew drank and the rats, sawdust, and oxhides they ate. A third group member related how it took Magellan 38 days to navigate through the rocky straits that later were named after him. The group also heard how he charted part of South America's west coast and how he was killed before he completed his mission.

Despite the short time allotted to the investigation, the children were exposed to a variety of source materials. The pictures of old compasses and other instruments that the maritime museum had sent the class circulated among the groups. Although the pictures were helpful, the children who chose to report on navigation did not fully understand how "astrolabes," "cross-staffs," and "knots" helped the mariners navigate. They were relieved to hear that the following week a scout master would come and explain how these and other instruments worked. Each group took time out to prepare a few questions to ask the "expert."

The group investigating Captain Cook met over the weekend at the home of one of the children to view the BBC videotape series on his expeditions. A member of another group brought a book of old maps of the world from the public library; the book made the rounds of all groups. One girl looked through her father's stamp collection and found Portugese stamps depicting fifteenth-century ships. These further illustrated what the children had learned from the brochures sent by the marine historical association.

During the last hour of the second session, each group put together all the individual members' reports and created a "passport" for the explorer they had investigated. The passports, which included the answers to the eight investigation questions, were photocopied so that each group member could have a copy.

Stage IV and Stage V: Groups Plan and Make Their Presentations

Mr. Garrett convened the whole class and explained that they would regroup in order to share what they had learned about explorers and then integrate their findings and present them to the class. "First, have everyone in your groups number off from 1 to 5. All 1's get together and form a new group, all 2's form a new group, and so on. Take your explorer's passport to your new group."

When the class settled down in their new groups, Mr. Garrett asked them to choose a chairperson to lead their discussions. Each chairperson got a card with the following instructions, which they all read to their groups:

1. Take turns reporting what each explorer discovered.
2. Based on these reports, discuss the ways these explorers changed the world.
3. Make a picture, chart, or table of your conclusions to show the class.

The children listened intently as the stories of the different explorers unfolded. After the reports, the discussions of the explorers' contributions began. Mr. Garrett distributed a large piece of oaktag, scissors, paste, and markers to all groups. As he circulated around the room, he heard animated conversations.

RAY: These men were really brave!

KEN: How could they spend so much time out on the ocean . . . days on end . . . not seeing land . . .

GINNY: They thought they knew where they were going . . .

RAY: They were sure they'd be rich, like Vasco da Gama.

ERIC: But they had such bad maps . . . and all that sickness . . .

KEN: Well, they helped make new maps, more accurate ones.

GINNY: That's one point we should write down, that the explorers changed the way people drew maps . . . I mean that maps became more accurate.

ERIC: Yeah, no more maps like we saw in that book without America on them.

TESSA: (chairperson) OK. We've got that point about the maps. How else did they change the world?

The children in this group continued to point out other areas of change. When it came time to decide how to present their conclusions to the class, they decided to draw a map of the explorers' routes. Each child drew a map of the routes traveled by the explorer he or she had specialized in. Together the children coordinated how to place the maps on the oaktag and where to write the appropriate names and dates.

One group deliberated about Cook's contribution to overcoming scurvy. Since he was the one to find the cure, the children felt that they could not ascribe that contribution to all five explorers. They solved their problem by deciding to make a table of the explorers and the specific ways they helped change the world. Each "expert" wrote about one explorer and his contribution on a strip of paper and pasted it on the oaktag. Another group also chose to make a table of the explorers and their contributions.

A fourth group presented its conclusions with pictures of each area in which the explorers influenced the world and short explanatory captions. Among them was a picture of the globe to illustrate that people learned that the world was round, a collage of pictures of foods and spices that explorers introduced to Europe, and pictures of people from the various countries the explorers encountered.

The fifth group divided their poster into three parts: new places, products, and routes. Under each part they wrote the appropriate details and then decorated the poster with pictures of maps, ships, and navigating instruments.

All posters were hung in the display area. One by one group representatives explained their posters to the class. Students commented on the clarity and appeal of each presentation.

Stage VI: Teacher and Students Evaluate Their Projects

Individual Evaluation.   Mr. Garrett borrowed an idea for individual evaluation from the explorers themselves and suggested that each student write a "diary." The students were asked to choose one phase of the explorer's life—such as a voyage, an encounter with a particular hardship, or the discovery of land—and describe it in diary form. They were told to include factual details as well as descriptions of what the explorers may have thought or felt. The completed diaries, with the teacher's comments, were placed in the display area so that anyone interested could read them.

Whole-Class Evaluation.   Each of the original study groups made up two questions about the explorer they had investigated. The class had one week to review the material and then took the test, which totaled ten questions, eight to be answered by each student. The study groups checked the answers to the questions they wrote, but Mr. Garrett graded the tests.

Wrap-Up.   At the end of the unit, Mr. Garrett asked for the class's comments on the process. The children's comments corroborated his impression that the process, although short, was stimulating. Joanne's comment was typical: "We had a great time, first in our study groups, then in the new groups . . . we got to teach each other in different ways, and it didn't seem like hard work at all."

WHAT MAKES A POEM A POEM?
A Tenth-Grade Study of Poetry

Mr. Baker was aware that students in his tenth-grade English class were uncomfortable with poetry. They thought that they could not understand it and were reluctant to try. Mr. Baker felt strongly that he should not teach poetry in any conventional way and therefore chose the following strategies: (1) responding aloud to poems in small group discussions (Dias 1979, 1985) and (2) Group Investigation. The first strategy served as an introduction to the unit. Students formed small groups at random and exchanged both their spontaneous reactions and their reflective responses to poems. Group Investigation provided the structure for creating their own repertoire of questions about poetry and for seeking the answers to these questions.

Even though both these strategies were new to the class, Mr. Baker was sure they would not be too strange or difficult. His students were used to conducting small-group discussions about short stories and novels and planning short-term assignments cooperatively.

Responding Aloud to Poems

The class was divided randomly into groups of four and five. For each of the four lessons the teacher chose a poem that allowed for a variety of thoughtful interpretations. Each group was asked to read the poem, discuss it, and report its interpretation to the class. Mr. Baker assured his students that they did not have to anticipate a specific line of inquiry or seek any "correct" answers. The poems were "It Is Dangerous to Read Newspapers" by Margaret Atwood, "Growin' Up" by Bruce Springsteen, "The Road Not Taken" by Robert Frost, and "Early Evening Quarrel" by Langston Hughes.

The procedure for group interpretation of the poems followed the steps suggested by Dias (1985), with some modifications. One member of each group was chosen to chair the discussion; another was chosen to be the presenter to the class.

The teacher distributed copies of the poem to each group so that each student had a copy. He read each poem aloud and asked if there were any particularly difficult or unfamiliar words. He explained the procedure for responding aloud and allotted them 20 minutes.

The leader of each group read the poem aloud, and then each group member read the poem silently. After the reading, each student in turn stated his or her initial reaction to the poem so that no ideas would be lost before the group discussion began. Students continued to comment on their observations, feelings, and general reactions to the poem. They were no longer required to speak in turn.

During the groups' discussions the teacher walked around the room to make sure that all group members participated in the discussion. One group seemed to reach an impasse in their discussion because they could not agree about the interpretation of the poem they were reading. Mr. Baker pointed out that there was really no need to reach an agreement and that it was perfectly legitimate for everyone to understand the poem in a different way. Following Dias's method, at no time did he volunteer an interpretation of his own.

Well into their discussion of Bruce Springsteen's "Growin' Up," one of the groups made the following comments:

DANNY: I can't understand everything he says, but I get the feeling that I know what he means.

JORGE:	What do you think he means?
DANNY:	Well, he seems to mean that he had a lot of pain . . .
MYRA:	Like he couldn't really find his place.
CATHLEEN:	But it says here that he got "a nice little place in the stars . . ."
JORGE:	Maybe . . . I guess that's after he lost everything he ever loved . . .
DANNY:	He went through so many different things before that. He "broke all the rules," but in the end he "stood up" and really stood out in the crowd.
MYRA:	That's really like his life . . . I mean his real life . . .

Each group deliberated about the main points of the poem they had read and decided what these were. They then made sure that the presenter was confident enough to share these ideas with the whole class. Each day a different group began reporting. Everyone in the class was welcome to participate in the classwide summary. Several groups felt that the words in the poems they read "let you see a lot of pictures in your mind" that made them want to read the poem again and again.

Stage I: Class Determines Subtopics and Organizes into Research Groups

First Lesson—Generating Questions.   Mr. Baker presented the general topic for investigation: "In the last four periods you read four poems and shared your reactions to them. These poems are very different from one another. These are only four examples of a rich and vast treasure of poetry the English-speaking world has produced. There are many more poems that we will read and enjoy, though we'll never read them all! But first I'd like you to think about what makes a poem a poem. You've gotten some ideas from the poems over the past four days. Think about what you would like to know in order to understand poetry. In buzz groups, think of all the questions that you'd like to explore. Don't forget to have one member write down all the questions that come up."

After 20 minutes, one group's recorder read his list of questions aloud and Mr. Baker wrote them down on the board. He then asked other recorders to read any questions on their lists that were not already on the board. From time to time he helped the students formulate their questions clearly.

The final list included the following questions:

1. When you write a poem, do you have to follow certain rules? How long should the lines be? Does a poem have to rhyme?
2. How come we can understand a poem written so long ago?
3. How come we can understand a poem written in a different country?
4. What do poems tell us about life at the time they were written?
5. Is there any right way to read a poem?
6. Can we learn about people's behavior from a poem?
7. Is there a difference between a song and a poem?
8. How much do we have to know about the historical background of the poem in order to understand it?
9. Do all societies have poets?
10. Why are poems considered so difficult to understand?
11. Does the reader have to understand every word in a poem?
12. When would a poet write a short poem? A long one? Does he choose the form of the poem before he writes it?

Mr. Baker asked the class to take a good look at the list of questions and see if they could sort them in any way into subtopics. After some discussion the class agreed on two subtopics:

a. What are the basic elements of poetry? Included were questions: 1, 2, 3, 5, 7, 10, 11, and 12.
b. How is the poet influenced by society and culture? Included were questions: 4, 6, 8, and 9. (There was a discussion whether questions 2 and 3 belong in this category. The class decided to leave it up to those who would choose this category.)

The lesson ended with Mr. Baker saying that next time everyone would choose which category he or she would like to pursue.

Second Lesson—Forming Investigation Groups. Mr. Baker placed on his desk a large collection of resource materials that the groups could use in addition to their textbook. He then hung two large posters on the wall, with the name of one subtopic on each. He invited the students to sign up for the subtopic of their choice. After every fifth name on the poster Mr. Baker drew a line to indicate that a new group was formed. When everyone decided which subtopic to investigate there were six groups of five students each and one group of six. Four groups were formed to investigate subtopic a, and three groups formed to investigate subtopic b.

At the close of this lesson, Mr. Baker presented the whole class with a general outline of Group Investigation. He showed the class a chart of each stage and explained briefly what was expected of the class in each one. The students were told that they could include in their inquiry the four poems used in the introductory lessons as well as any other poems they chose from the resource materials. They had four English periods to plan and carry out their investigation. In addition, each student was expected to write an individual paper responding to a poem of his or her choice. Mr. Baker handed out the guidelines for this assignment (for details of the assignment see stage VI, below). These papers would be part of each student's final grade.

Stage II: Groups Plan Their Investigations

The first item on each group's agenda was to review the study questions and decide if there were any other questions they wanted to add. The next step was to divide the questions among group members and to assign roles. Each group chose a coordinator and a recorder. They also chose one member to represent them on the steering committee, which would meet at a later date.

Afterwards, each group discussed the resources they would use in their investigations. One member of each group went to Mr. Baker's desk to choose a few books and magazines to help them get started.

One student in a group that had chosen to study the elements of poetry invited his groupmates to his home to view the movie *Dead Poets Society*. He had not seen it yet, but he thought it would be fun to find out if it could shed light on their topic. In another group, one student volunteered to bring all the materials her parents had collected on their visit the past summer to Dove Cottage, Wordsworth's home in England. She was sure it would help them understand how the poet's environment had influenced his poetry.

By the end of the period each group had filled out two copies of the group planning form. One copy was posted on the wall and the other was kept by the group's chairperson.

Stage III: Groups Carry Out Their Investigations

Three periods were set aside for groups to seek answers to their questions and formulate conclusions. In some groups students divided the questions among themselves so that each student concentrated on a different aspect of the subtopic. In other groups all the students looked up material relevant to all the questions.

As the teacher circulated among the groups in the second period, he heard one group, which was investigating subtopic a, raise the issue of rhyme as well as the connection between a song and a poem. Here is an excerpt from their discussion:

LINDA: Well, it seems that all poems don't rhyme. I read a few in this anthology, and they don't all rhyme.

SEAN: I read all of Springsteen's songs; some rhyme and some don't. Some even have only two lines rhyming . . . the rest don't.

ALLAN: Well, it's hard to tell, did he write the music first or the words first?

LINDA: Are we sure that he writes real poetry? Does he write poems or songs?

ARNIE: A song is a poem set to music, isn't it? I asked my aunt, who teaches English, about poetry, and she told me that the beginning of poetry was music. Music and words weren't split apart. Like in ancient Greece . . . those long epic poems were chanted.

ALLAN: I guess that made them easy to remember.

MR. BAKER: You know, in ancient times there was no prose. That's one of the things we'll learn about later on this year. Meanwhile, though, read Langston Hughes's poem again and see if it reminds you of a song, and if so, why. [He made a note to return to this group and see what they concluded about the connections between songs and poems.]

Mr. Baker saw another group, investigating subtopic b, hunched over the brochures and photographs of Dove Cottage:

AVIVA: Here's the room where he sat . . . he had a special room for writing . . . and look at those beautiful hills . . . it says that he loved to go on long walks . . .

ANAT: Can you understand his poems? They're so long!

AVIVA: Well, I guess I really don't understand them, and I didn't really read them, but there's one poem that I read and could make out, about the daffodils he sees on his walks. You want to hear it? [She read the poem aloud.]

JOHN:	So, can we say that poets write about what they see around them?
MIKE:	At least we know that Wordsworth did. What about Langston Hughes? Doesn't seem like he was influenced by nature.
ANAT:	But he wrote about the kind of *people* he saw around him . . .
MR. BAKER:	Well, you see, each of those poets lived in such a different environment, and it seems to me that their poems tell you a lot about how they lived.
JOHN:	Then any society can have a poet.
MR. BAKER:	That's right! And all societies do have poets . . .

Mr. Baker went on to another group, which was investigating subtopic a and had decided to divide the questions among them. Two students were discussing questions 10 and 11: "Why are poems considered so difficult to understand?" and "Does the reader have to understand every word in a poem?" Ted seemed quite frustrated.

TED:	Poems are difficult to understand because the poets use such different words!
RACHEL:	Maybe because they write about what *they* see and feel, not about what other people see and feel.
TED:	Well, I know they're not newspaper reporters . . . but they want you to read what they write . . .
RACHEL:	I wonder if they want you to understand *every word* they write.
TED:	If they don't want you to understand them, then why do they write them to begin with?
MR. BAKER:	You know, that gives me an idea. How about interviewing a poet and asking him or her those questions? I'll arrange for you to meet one of the poets I know . . .

Ted and Rachel asked the poet all their questions. He explained that poetry should be approached differently than prose and that poets know that not everyone will understand what they write.

By the end of the third period (of this stage) all groups had completed their inquiry. They discussed the answers to the questions they had set out to investigate and summarized them in writing. Mr. Baker read each summary and returned them to the groups with his comments. Groups spent the next period correcting their reports and then posted them on the wall, alongside the group planning form. Some reports were in the form of a list of answers to the questions, others were in essay form.

Stage IV: Groups Plan Their Presentations

At the beginning of the next period, each group spent half an hour generating ideas for their presentations. Mr. Baker then met with the steering committee, while the rest of the class began working on the individual papers that Mr. Baker had assigned in the second lesson of stage I. The representative of each group reported on the ideas they had for the presentations of their findings to the class. Danny, who represented the group that had viewed the movie *Dead Poets Society*, thought the whole class should see it. He told the committee that the movie convinced his group that poetry can have a strong emotional impact on people. The representative from Ted's group told the committee how much the whole group learned from Ted and Rachel's meeting with a poet. This aroused the interest of other committee members, who felt that it was worthwhile inviting the poet to meet with the whole class.

Finally, the steering committee decided that the class would put together its own "anthology" that would include each group's summary as well as their individual papers. In addition, each group would prepare questions for the poet and choose a member to serve on a panel that would interview him. The committee decided to have Danny explain to the class why seeing the movie was worthwhile.

Stage V: Groups Make Their Presentations

The "presentations" in this Group Investigation were not of the conventional kind, where each group presents the essence of its findings to the class. In this case the whole class participated in the interview, so that the questions they asked reflected what they had learned as well as what they wanted to know.

The interview with the poet was scheduled for the following week. In the meantime, Mr. Baker photocopied the six group summaries and distributed them to all the students. These summaries served as additional resource material for each student's individual paper, which they worked on during the week.

The morning of the interview the class rearranged the room so the chairs formed two concentric circles. The poet and the group representatives sat in the inner circle. At first, he told the class how he had come to write poetry and what he felt were the main influences on his writing. Then he invited each group's representative to ask a few questions. Many of the questions were the same that the class had set out to investigate. The students were curious to hear how a "real live" poet answered them.

Toward the end of the session, the poet summed up by saying:

> Well, I can tell that you've all learned a lot about what makes a poem a poem. It's really hard to analyze the elements of a poem without losing the essence of poetry. Maybe a good way of summing it up is that what makes a poem a poem is the language the poet uses, together with the pictures the poem brings to mind and the feelings the language and pictures arouse in the reader . . . and I really don't always know what comes first. In fact, sometimes I get the idea for a poem in a dream! Anyway, a poem should always help you see and feel things in a new way. I wish you lots of luck in your adventure, as you read more poems throughout the year. I hope you"ll also try writing some yourselves. You'll see that anyone and everyone can write poetry.

Stage VI: Teacher and Students Evaluate Their Projects

Individual Evaluation. The individual evaluation was based on the paper each student wrote. Mr. Baker had handed out the following guidelines for this paper:

- Choose a poem and describe why you like it. Are there any words that arouse special feelings? What pictures do the words make you see?
- Write a short paragraph about the poet's life and environment.
- Explain how, in your opinion, the poet's life and environment are connected to his or her poetry.
- What is the most interesting thing about poetry that you learned in this project?

Whole-Class Evaluation. For the whole-class evaluation of the Group Investigation project, Mr. Baker asked the students to discuss the question "In what way did conducting a Group Investigation help you learn about poetry?" The discussion began in pairs. After ten minutes, Mr. Baker asked each pair to exchange their views with another pair. Ten minutes later he reconvened the whole class and asked who would like to share their reactions with the class? Some of the students' reactions were:

> "I had plenty of time to get used to the idea that poems aren't weird or too hard to understand."
>
> "At first it was hard to know exactly what to look for, but I got used to it and the kids in my group helped a lot."
>
> "I liked the fact that I could choose what to read about poetry and didn't have to stick to the textbook."
>
> "Hearing all those ideas in my group really opened my eyes to what makes a poem a poem. I see that there's so much to know about language and the background of the poet . . . I enjoyed it very much."
>
> "I'm glad we had to do an individual paper because it helped me put everything together."
>
> "I think you should go over the groups' summaries with us. I read them all, but I didn't understand them all."
>
> "Without Group Investigation we would have just read the book and heard you. This way we could talk about what interested us, and we interviewed the poet, and we read different books . . . it was more interesting."
>
> "Actually, we found the answers to our own questions. We never did that before . . . it was pretty exciting, though in the beginning I didn't really believe we could do it."

Mr. Baker could not help feeling satisfied that through Group Investigation his students had gained new understandings of the elements of poetry as well as confidence and interest in reading poetry. He looked forward to exploring more poems with them during the year. The groups' summaries and students' individual papers gave him a great deal of information about what the students had actually learned about poetry and which elements he should emphasize in the future.

"WHAT DO STAMPS TEACH US ABOUT THE UNITED STATES?"
A Fourth-Grade Group Investigation Project

Stamps are an intriguing introduction to places, events, and people both near and far, known and unknown. Ms. Sherman felt that a class stamp collection would be an appropriate stimulus for Group Investigation because of its diverse content and its appeal to children. The stamps would serve as an initial source of information, which would lead the children to explore a wide variety of subjects and expand their ability to find answers to their questions.

The children were invited to bring stamps to the classroom and place them in a "mailbox" that Ms. Sherman made out of cardboard. She also asked other teachers to contribute to the class's collection. A few teachers were curious as to what she planned to do with them, so Ms. Sherman promised to show them the results at the end of the project.

Ms. Sherman prepared a learning station where children could work individually or in pairs. She knew from past experience that not all groups would conduct their investigations at the same pace. Those who were waiting for others to complete their work in a particular stage of the project could in the meantime work at the station. The activity cards at the station dealt with the basic features of stamps and taught the children how to remove stamps from envelopes and put them in an album. There were also arithmetic problems based on the monetary value of different stamps.

The growing number of stamps in the class's collection aroused the children's curiosity and stimulated them to ask many questions about their design as well as their content. On their own the children began to classify the stamps according to countries of origin.

Stage I: Class Determines Subtopics and Organizes into Research Groups

Two weeks after the collection began, Ms. Sherman introduced the Group Investigation. She presented the general topic "What do stamps teach us about the United States?"

Forming Study Groups. The class's first task was to sort the U.S. stamps into subtopics. Groups were formed at random, and Ms. Sherman distributed the stamps among them. Each group received magnifying glasses, which helped them look at details. It was not long before a representative of each group went up to the board and wrote the group's suggested list of topics. Ms. Sherman asked each one to look at what the others had written so as not to repeat a topic. When the lists were completed, the children decided which topics they would like to pursue. Ms. Sherman explained that they did not have to choose all the topics on the board. The class chose the following six topics, and study groups were formed according to the children's interests (Figure 5.3):

- Presidents (5 children)
- U.S. flag (4 children)
- Christmas (2 children)
- Air Mail (3 children)
- Centennials (6 children)
- Conservation (5 children)

Ms. Sherman gave each group a box for the stamps in their category. The children spent the last few minutes of the session choosing a chairperson and a recorder for each group. The recorders wrote the group's subtopic and the names of the group members on a poster, under the title: "What do stamps teach us about the United States?" Ms. Sherman decorated the poster by pasting stamps all around it. She used stamps that had messages on them, such as "Greetings," "Love You, Dad!" and "Love You, Mother!" as well as cancellations with messages such as "Fall in love with stamp collecting."

In order to establish continuity in the investigation, Ms. Sherman set aside two consecutive hours a week for the project. The whole project lasted two months.

Stage II: Groups Plan Their Investigations

The following week Ms. Sherman handed each group a sheet of instructions:

1. Look at the stamps carefully: What can you learn from them? What do the words tell you? What do the pictures tell you?
2. What else would you like to know about the person, place, or event on the stamps?
3. Where will you find the answers? Write down all the places, books, and people who might be of help.
4. Decide how you will find the information you need and divide the work among yourselves.

The children began examining their stamps. With the help of magnifying glasses, they noticed the different details on each stamp. Gradually they began to ask questions about what they saw. There

Figure 5.3   What Do Stamps Teach Us about the United States?

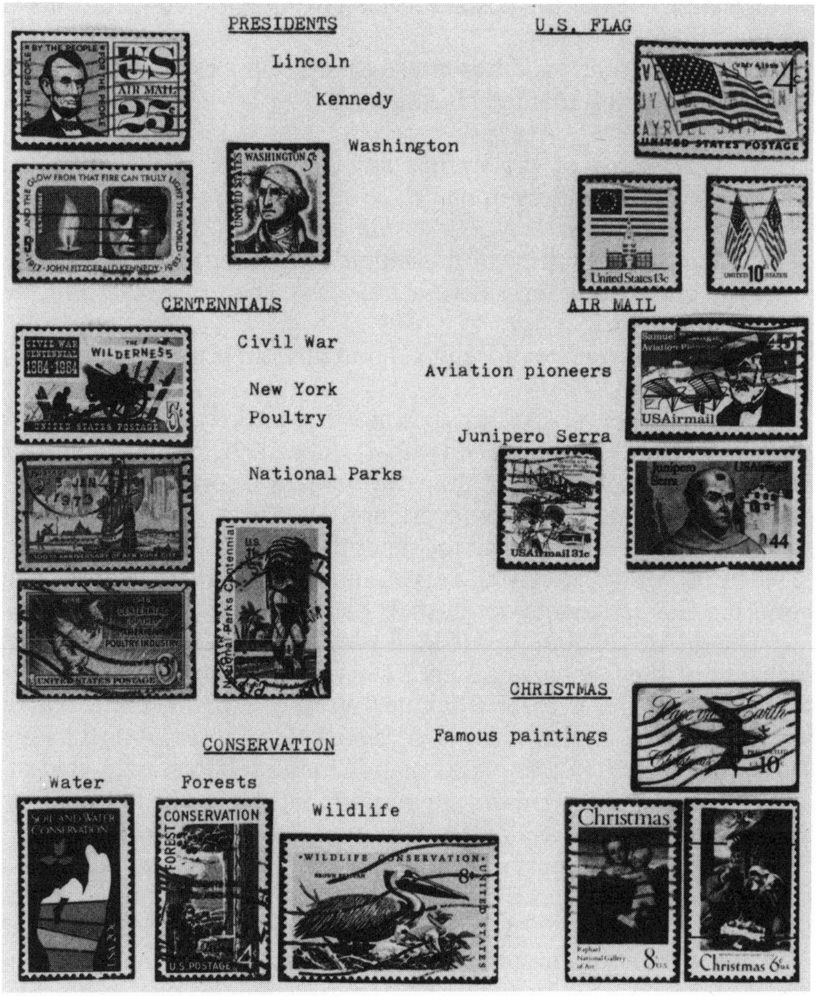

PRESIDENTS
Lincoln
Kennedy
Washington

U.S. FLAG

CENTENNIALS
Civil War
New York
Poultry
National Parks

AIR MAIL
Aviation pioneers
Junipero Serra

CHRISTMAS
Famous paintings

CONSERVATION
Water   Forests
Wildlife

were words to look up, dates to clarify, people, places, and institutions to identify.

By the end of the hour all groups had compiled a list of questions. The chairperson in each group suggested they divide among them the topics depicted on the stamps. Some groups decided to spend the next hour in the school library, looking up basic facts about their respective subtopics. Ms. Sherman suggested that they see if the library had a copy of the postal service's catalog, which would answer many of their questions.

The group that had chosen presidents as its topic decided upon the following questions for investigation:

> Why do some of the stamps have the dates of the president's term and others don't?
>
> Does every president get a stamp in his honor?
>
> Do they issue stamps of presidents only after they're dead?
>
> How come some presidents have more than one stamp in their honor?
>
> Why do the stamps of Kennedy and Lincoln print what they said?

One member of the group was very interested in finding the sources of the quotations on the stamps depicting Kennedy and Lincoln. Three children wanted to look up information about the presidents depicted in the other stamps. Another volunteered to make a list of all the presidents and the dates they served. They also planned to write to the U.S. Postal Service and ask if there were stamps honoring the presidents not in their collection.

The group examining Air Mail stamps planned to interview the manager of the local post office. A few children in the group decided to investigate the lives of Chanute, Wright, Langley, and Sikorsky, whose pictures appeared on a series devoted to aviation pioneers. They were sure they'd find information in the school library, and they also accepted Ms. Sherman's suggestion that they write to the Air and Space Museum in Washington, D.C., for additional information.

Many of the stamps depicting the U.S. flag showed examples of flags from the eighteenth century, including a stamp of the first stars and stripes. Two children in this group planned to find out how and why the number of the stars and stripes changed over the years. They assumed they would find information in the encyclopedia. Ms. Sherman recommended that they also ask the chairperson of the history department. Two other members of the group were intrigued by stamps depicting a flag flying over a building. They planned to find out what these buildings were and what they had to do with the flag (they recognized the White House). One child said they could start by looking in a guidebook of Washington, D.C., that he would bring from home.

There were not many stamps in the conservation collection, but they were almost equally divided into the various aspects of conservation: water, wildlife, forest, range, and soil. Each child chose one area of conservation. Unfortunately, the stamps did not provide any clues as to where to look for information on what conservation is all about. Ms. Sherman suggested that they write to the Department of Agriculture as well as to the World Wildlife Fund. She pointed out that while they were waiting for an answer they could speak to the science teacher.

The stamps in the Christmas collection depicted famous paintings displayed in the National Gallery of Art. Visiting the gallery was impossible, but the children were curious to learn of other paintings on the subject of Christmas. Both children's parents were enlisted to take them to the local art museum over the weekend.

Stage III: Groups Carry Out Their Investigations

During the week the children wrote letters to the various institutions on their list of resources. While the children waited for replies to their letters, some looked up information in various reference books in the school library and others interviewed different "experts."

As the investigation progressed, the children discovered new sources of information. The school librarian showed the group investigating centennials a videotape about national parks. The tape was informative as well as beautiful; and since it stressed the importance of caring for the parks, the children suggested that the conservation group see it, too.

Before their visit to the post office, children studying Air Mail stamps made up a list of questions to ask the manager:

Why are there special stamps marked Air Mail?
When were the first special stamps for Air Mail issued? (They had a stamp marking the fiftieth anniversary of U.S. Air Mail service with no dates on it.)
Why are there Air Mail stamps with pictures of people that have nothing to do with air mail, like the stamp with Junipero Serra's picture?
Why does the post office give you an Air Mail sticker as well as the stamp?

After the interview, the manager volunteered to come and talk to the whole class. He was very eager to meet the children and answer their questions, since this was the first time he had heard about a whole class using stamps for their work. He donated several catalogs of new stamps from the Philatelic Sales Division, which all the groups found useful.

Some of the children in the conservation group found postcards and pictures at home from family trips to several national parks. The group's leader asked the rest of the class to bring any pictures they might have from trips they had taken.

By the fourth week of the investigation, several groups received answers to their letters that included a great deal of new material. The number of flyers, leaflets, and posters grew and enriched the information they were getting from the references in the school library. Those who were still waiting for replies worked at the learning station Ms. Sherman had prepared.

The visit to the art museum proved fascinating to the two children in the Christmas group, and they asked to go a second time. The paintings aroused their imaginations, and they decided to draw their own stamps of Christmas scenes, complete with monetary value. While they were drawing, they talked about the possibility of making an album of their set of Christmas stamps, with accompanying stories.

Groups Integrate Their Findings.   During the fifth week of the investigation, Ms. Sherman asked the groups to organize their findings and integrate them. They were to summarize what they had learned about the people, events, and places on their stamps and to conclude why they were important enough to be shown on a stamp.

The first hour was spent in animated discussions. Group members read the results of their interviews to one another, shared the information they had gathered, and looked again at the pictures and leaflets they had received. By the second hour most groups were ready to write their summaries.

Ms. Sherman circulated among the groups. Halfway into the first hour, the chairperson of the group that had studied about presidents asked for her help. They could not seem to integrate the information they had gathered.

DICK:	(chairperson) Everybody did their work and we got a lot of information, but we don't know how to summarize it all.
PAT:	We know that all the presidents are important.
GARY:	Well, some are more important than others. I

think there are more stamps of Lincoln and
Washington and Kennedy than of other presidents.

BECKY: Should we write about each president?

JUDI: I have a list of all the presidents and the years
they were presidents.

DICK: What about Washington? The father of our
country . . .

MS. SHERMAN: What you said about the fact that there are
more stamps of some presidents than others
seems like a good point. Why not think about
that? Why do you think some may be more important than others?

GARY: OK . . . maybe we'll write about Kennedy and
Lincoln.

DICK: We have a lot of information about them.

MS. SHERMAN: What makes them important? Try to think
about that first and then think about Washington. Take turns saying what you think.

The group's leader asked each member in turn to say why he or
she thought Kennedy and Lincoln were important to the nation. By
the second round they had begun to clarify their ideas and saw that
they could be summarized in a few sentences. They called Ms. Sherman over, and she encouraged them to continue discussing their
ideas about the other presidents. By the end of the two hours this
group had succeeded in summarizing their ideas about why it is
important to have stamps that depict the various presidents.

At the end of the second hour Ms. Sherman told the class that the
following week would be devoted to planning their presentations. She
reminded each group to choose one child to serve on the steering
committee, which would coordinate all their plans for the presentations.

Stage IV: Groups Plan Their Presentations

Ms. Sherman began with a whole-class discussion about the
different ways the groups might present their findings. She encouraged the children to think of presentations that would highlight the
reasons all their subtopics were chosen to be depicted on stamps.

The discussion concluded with the following plans:

1. A few children in each group would prepare a display of the group's major findings.
2. Six children, one from each group, would get together to prepare the class's "philatelic catalog," containing the groups' summaries. They would write a quiz about each display to add to the catalog.
3. The steering committee would plan the schedule of visitors to the exhibit as well as the schedule for student guides.
4. Ms. Sherman would be in charge of photocopying the catalog.

The following hour each group began planning its display. At the end of the day Ms. Sherman heard members of the steering committee report their groups' plans. They decided to invite the principal to the opening of the exhibit and coordinated the schedule for the parents' visit as well as the other fourth grade's visit. They also planned to prepare a visitors' book with room for comments. The groups' plans were quite diverse, and they spent the following week carrying them out.

Presidents.   The children prepared a poster of all the stamps in their collection, with a short summary about each president. Around the border of the poster they carefully printed the quotations from the Kennedy and the Lincoln stamps. The full chart of all the presidents was pasted underneath.

U.S. Flag.   Two children prepared a poster of the eight stamps they had that showed the different flags used in the 1770s. The last stamp was the first stars and stripes. They wrote an explanatory caption under each flag. One child drew a diagram showing how the number of stars in the flag had changed over the years.

Christmas.   By this time the two children in this group had an impressive number of stamps and stories to put in their holiday album. An enlargement of the "Peace on Earth" stamp served as the cover. This was followed by the four stamps with famous paintings, one on each page, with a few sentences explaining the event depicted in the painting. Next came their own stamps and stories. Until the album was completed, no one was allowed to peek—not even Ms. Sherman.

Air Mail.   The children in this group borrowed an idea from one of their stamps and used a large map of the world as the background of their poster. They pasted their Air Mail stamps all over the map to illustrate how Air Mail connects the U.S. with other countries. Two children made another poster with stamps of the aviation pioneers and added captions about their major contributions to the field. The third member of the group prepared a display of all the material they received from the manager of the post office.

Conservation.   Under the title "Preserve the Environment," the children pasted the stamps depicting each of the five aspects of conservation they had studied. They surrounded them with the post-cards and photographs they had collected. On a separate chart they displayed material they had received from the Department of Agriculture about the importance of conservation.

Centennials.   This group chose to display the diverse subtopics of their investigation in chronological order. They made a chart of their stamps, with the dates of the centennials written alongside. They added one line about the significance of each centennial. With the help of the teacher in charge of computers, two group members prepared a quiz about the Civil War (one of the centennials). Visitors to the exhibit would call it up on the class's computer and answer the questions. Each one would receive a printout to keep.

The Class's Catalog.   Ms. Sherman convened this group one afternoon to work on the class's own "philatelic catalog." The catalog consisted of six pages, one for each group's summary. On the cover of the catalog they wrote the title of the Group Investigation project and drew a picture of a group of children examining stamps. At the end of the catalog they wrote a quiz for the visitors. The quiz consisted of two questions for each display. The catalog was photocopied so that there were enough copies for every class member and for all potential visitors to the exhibit.

Stage V: Groups Make Their Presentations

The morning of the opening of the class's stamp exhibit, the children came early and helped arrange all the desks on one side of the room. Copies of the class's "philatelic catalog" were placed on the desks for distribution to all visitors. The teacher positioned a TV monitor in between the displays of the centennial and conservation groups so that the tape on national parks could be viewed in connection with both these topics. The conservation group also brought slide viewers so that visitors could see slides children had brought of their trips to some of the parks. The Christmas album was placed on a separate table with all sorts of Christmas decorations. A large sign was placed on top of the computer to draw visitors' attention to the quiz.

The children were thrilled when the principal officially "opened" the exhibit by cutting the ribbon Ms. Sherman had tied across the door. The first visitors were the children from the other fourth grade. Each group member had a turn serving as a guide to his or her group's display while other group members toured the exhibit. As they went from one display to the next, all the children filled out the quiz at the back of the catalog. After lunch the parents came and viewed the exhibit with great pride. Each visitor, children and parents alike, was invited to write comments in the visitors' book.

Stage VI: Teacher and Students Evaluate Their Projects

The visitors' comments served as a very welcome kind of evaluation, as did the growing interest in the exhibit shown by other grades. The class had to plan another day hosting other classes. During the week they wrote thank-you letters to all the people and institutions that had helped them with their research.

To wrap up the project, Ms. Sherman asked the class to discuss what they enjoyed most about the project and what they felt they had learned from it. Their comments focused on the fun they had had looking up so many different topics that they did not normally associate with school. As a result of their experience, they saw how much of what they had learned touched upon what they were studying in their "regular" lessons. A few children announced that they had begun collecting stamps and subscribed to the Postal Service's catalog. Ms. Sherman pointed out how they all had refined their ability to locate information and integrate their findings.

Ms. Sherman did not forget her promise, and at the next staff meeting she reported on the project to her colleagues. She emphasized how the stamps had stimulated the children to inquire into a great variety of subjects and how Group Investigation structured the process of inquiry so that individuals and groups achieved their goals.

The projects are summarized in Table 5.1 for easy comparison. When read from left to right the table shows how each project unfolded stage by stage. When read vertically, the table highlights the

Table 5.1 Four Group Investigation Projects

General Topic of Investigation; Grade and Content Area	Why Did the Teacher Choose Group Investigation?	Stage I: a) Classwide Organization and Planning How Did the Teacher Introduce Group Investigation?
Grade 3 Science: "What and How Do Animals Eat?" Part of the science curriculum	To give class experience in learning from a wide range of sources and in planning what to study.	The whole class visited the zoo at feeding time.
Grade 6 Geography: "How Did Explorers Change the World?" Expanding a unit on Columbus	Group Investigation offers students choice of explorers they want to study in depth.	Whole class studied about Columbus's voyages and discoveries and how they changed the concept of the world at the time.
Grade 10 English: "What Makes a Poem a Poem?" A unit on poetry	Group Investigation involves students in directly investigating basic elements of poetry.	Teacher supplied four poems of different authors; students responded to poems spontaneously.
Grade 4 Extracurricular: "What Can Stamps Teach Us About the United States?"	Use of stamps as a unique stimulus for inquiry; content of Group Investigation completely determined by classification of stamps.	Class collected stamps for two weeks.

Table 5.1 (continued)

Stage I: b) Classwide Organization and Planning Cooperative Planning of Subtopics for Investigation	Stage II: Each Group Plans Its Investigation
Teacher led whole class in cooperative planning of questions for inquiry.	Each group chose one class of animals.
All groups investigated the same questions, but each group investigated a different class of animals.	Each group member investigated a different animal in that class.
Cooperative planning of questions by pairs, foursomes, and whole class. Each group investigated same questions, but about a different explorer.	Group members divided questions among themselves and sought answers from different sources.
Cooperative planning of questions by "buzz" groups yielded two subtopics. Study groups formed on basis of interest in subtopic.	Group members sought answers from different sources. Some groups divided the questions among themselves; others divided the materials but not the questions.
Cooperative planning of subtopics by whole class. Interest groups formed; planned their questions for investigation.	Each group organized its investigation in a different way: They planned interviews and site visits, decided which resource material to read, and wrote letters to experts. Questions and resources were divided among group members.

General Topic of Investigation; Grade and Content Area	Stage III: All Groups Carry Out Their Plans	Stage IV: Groups Plan Their Presentations
Grade 3 Science: "What and How Do Animals Eat?" Part of the science curriculum	Individual plus group study of study questions. Group summary of individuals' findings.	Groups prepared a "TV documentary" or a quiz. One group prepared a game for the class.
Grade 6 Geography: "How Did Explorers Change the World?" Expanding a unit on Columbus	All group members gathered information from a variety of sources; each student reported to his or her group; the group summarized the explorer's characteristics and contributions.	Each group prepared a "passport" for the explorer it had investigated. Each group planned how to present the "passport" to reconstituted groups.
Grade 10 English: "What Makes a Poem a Poem?" A unit on poetry	Students read a variety of sources; saw a film; interviewed a poet. Each group prepared a written summary of its conclusions.	The steering committee decided to invite the poet for a classwide interview. Each group prepared a few questions for the interview.
Grade 4 Extracurricular: "What Can Stamps Teach Us About the United States?"	Students wrote letters, visited sites, interviewed experts, read a variety of resource materials. Each group integrated its findings.	Each group prepared its part for the classwide exhibit. They wrote stories and prepared posters, diagrams, slides, drawings, and a computer quiz.

Table 5.1 (continued)

Stage V: Groups Present Their Findings	Stage VI: Evaluation
Some groups presented their "documentary"; others presented a quiz. Game was available for all students.	The teacher met with each group separately to discuss how they worked together, how they organized their work, what they liked best about it, and what difficulties they had. The teacher led a classwide summary of what the class learned about conducting Group Investigation. Individual grade based on worksheet.
Reconstituted groups heard a report of each explorer's life and contributions. Each group discussed and summarized how all the explorers changed the way people saw the world.	The teacher gave the class a written quiz, to which each study group contributed two questions about their explorer. Students wrote individual essays in the form of an explorer's diary.
Class interviewed a local poet.	Individual grade based on an analysis of a poem
Class prepared an "anthology" of the groups' summaries and their individual papers.	Classwide evaluation of how Group Investigation helped understand the elements that "make a poem a poem."
Classwide exhibit included slides, albums, a videotape, and the class' own philatelic catalog.	Class reflects on process of investigating in groups.
Parents and other classes were scheduled to attend at different times.	All visitors to the exhibit wrote comments in the "visitors' book."

variety of ways in which each stage was carried out as well as the diverse reasons teachers had for choosing Group Investigation.

A PET PROJECT
A High School Group Investigation Project

Group Investigation can be applied in a variety of contexts. It can be expanded to achieve broad social and educational goals not limited exclusively to the study of academic topics. In the following example Group Investigation is employed as part of a very broad project based in the school but closely tied to community settings. The project was undertaken and directed by a team of teachers working closely with students' parents and with representatives of various community organizations.

The Pet Project grew out of a series of discussions held by the principal and a group of teachers of a high school with representatives of a wide range of community organizations, both private and public. The main focus of these discussions was to understand the community's problem with providing teenagers with attractive and positive social experiences after school hours as well as to help them avoid entanglement in antisocial activities. After many meetings it became clear that activities outside school could be better understood if they were viewed as continuous with the nature of the experiences that students have in school. The less separation there was between these two parts of the students' experience, the greater chance they stood of coming to grips with the challenge of creating successful programs for youth. Indeed, this conclusion was precisely what John Dewey had observed at the end of the last century (see Chapter 1).

This insight led, first and foremost, to having the school, in cooperation with community representatives, develop programs that incorporated a high level of interest on the part of both the students and the community in the substance of the program, as well as a high level of active involvement of the students in community life (Sarason, 1983; Sarason, Caroll, Maton, Cohen, & Lorentz, 1977; Sarason & Lorentz, 1979). Clearly, commercial settings were a central focus of community life. With this thought in mind, the Pet Project was born.

In the school, a team was formed that included teachers of biology, home economics, accounting, and general science, as well as the guidance teacher and an assistant principal. They reached several policy decisions regarding the Pet Project. First, students would be given formal credit for their contribution to the project, both in and out of school. Second, parental participation wherever possible was imperative for the success of the project. Third, students would be asked to submit periodic reports on their work, and the teachers would meet with the students at regular intervals to discuss the general implications of the project. Fourth, part of the project would be carried out during school hours, which required coordination with the students' class schedules, and part of the project would require that students invest their time after school hours. Finally, it was obvious to the teachers that such a project must continue for a relatively long time in order to reap its potential benefits. It was decided that the same students would pursue the project for two academic years.

The essence of the Pet Project was that several classes of tenth- and eleventh-grade students undertook to raise, care for, and market animals ordinarily sold in pet shops. They had to study and understand all the complexities involved in this project, including the animals' biology and ecology, their nutrition, their health and habits, the optimal conditions for their preservation and growth before sale to pet shops, the marketing of the pets to shops, transportation of the animals, and all of the bookkeeping and accounting required. The wide range of animals found in pet shops also demanded that the students acquire a great deal of knowledge. Stores typically sold not only many kinds of dogs, cats, birds, turtles, and fish but also snakes, small monkeys, guinea pigs of different kinds, and so forth. It was obvious to teachers and students alike that there was a lot to learn before they began the project and during its implementation.

It was here that the Group Investigation approach to learning served the purposes of this project. The Pet Project followed the general guidelines of Group Investigation, even though the stages were implemented somewhat differently from the previous examples in this chapter.

The Group Investigation Project

Classwide Organization and Planning. The students were involved from the start in planning the implementation of this project. Obviously, since everyone could not master every aspect of this complex project, teams of students were formed on the basis of their interest in particular aspects of the work.

Group Planning.   Teams generally specialized in at least two major components of the work, such as ecology and transportation, or nutrition and accounting, but, through a variety of methods, all students were required to learn more about all aspects of the project. Moreover, the students decided that, even though their original groups were formed on the basis of their interest in particular features of the project, group membership could change if they wished. Groups would also rotate in terms of the areas of their responsibility when they felt they had completed a significant term of work in a given area.

Investigation.   The first three months of the project were spent investigating all the features of the project that the students, with the teachers' assistance, identified as vital. Students gathered information from pet shop owners, from publications of local and state governments regulating the care and sale of animals, and, of course, from articles and books listed on bibliographies prepared, in large part, by the teachers. There were many films available from public libraries, from the SPCA, government agencies, and private groups concerned with the care of animals. Students cooperated in deciding where to go to obtain information and how to divide the material among themselves.

Planning Presentations.   Groups planned how to prepare reports based on the different sources of information. Reports were of many different kinds, some oral, others typed and circulated among all the groups; still others consisted of collections of photographs, brochures, and so forth with captions highlighting important pieces of information.

Steering Committees.   To facilitate the management of this project, the students and teachers decided to maintain three steering committees. One committee dealt with the "academic" aspects of the project, such as the groups' study of the animals. The second committee concerned itself with all the problems related to the storage and care of the animals in the school. The third committee coordinated all of the community-related aspects of the project, such as establishing extensive contacts with pet shop owners, determining and monitoring the cost of raising the animals, determining the sale price of each kind of animal in relation to costs, arranging for the rental of delivery trucks, and so forth. Each steering committee represented several smaller groups of students whose job it was to deal with specific topics. Thus the steering committees were simultaneously able to coordinate the work of all the groups and keep track of the groups' progress. The teachers responsible for the project also maintained close contact with one another through a schedule of team meetings. Work on the delivery of animals to stores was done in close cooperation with parents. Parents were also involved in other aspects of the project as well, depending upon their interests and skills.

Implementation.   The investigation of the topic and the presentation of each group's findings constituted a necessary stage of preparation for the actual implementation of the project. Unlike other Group Investigation projects, the investigation itself was not identical with the implementation stage. Moreover, presentation of the groups' work had to precede the stage of implementation.

Gradually, the equipment for storing and caring for the animals was assembled, and toward the second half of the year the students and teachers felt they had learned enough to begin implementing the project. Implementation was very gradual, in terms of both the animals that were raised and sold and the number of pet shop owners to whom the animals were sold. Over the summer, many students, with the help of their parents, invested a great deal of time and energy in promoting the project. During the second year the project was expanded greatly and began to make a profit from the sale of the animals.

Evaluation.   Throughout the year and a half during which the same students pursued this project, the teacher team conducted meetings of the various classes in order to keep everyone informed on progress and problems. This class meeting was a convenient arena for monitoring and evaluating the contribution of each group to the project.

The teachers felt that the knowledge and experience gained by the students went far beyond anything they would have learned had the subjects related to this project been taught in the traditional manner. On their part, students said it was one of the most unforgettable experiences of their entire school career. Some examinations were given in such areas as animal biology, ecology, nutrition, and accounting in order to provide school authorities with a formal check on students' academic knowledge of these topics, but in general the teachers knew exactly what students had accomplished and who had invested effort in this work.

The Pet Project was continued subsequently by new classes entering the tenth and eleventh grades, when the original tenth-graders were in the twelfth grade and the original eleventh-graders had graduated. But it was only one of several such community-based projects conducted by the high schools in this county. Other projects had a totally different character. One concentrated on local history and family roots (a subject popular in many schools for which the Group Investigation method is particularly suited); another focused on the role of insurance companies in community life, with particular emphasis on the study of the statistics and mathematics employed by insurance companies. This latter project was carried out with the close collaboration of several large insurance companies whose home offices were located in the area.

The character of investigation projects combined with community-centered activities that can be carried out by high schools, all with great demands on students (and teachers) for acquiring extensive knowledge and for investing time in some work in the community, depends to a large extent on the imagination of the school's teaching staff (McClure, Cook, & Thompson, 1977). Clearly, it also requires the school's willingness to depart from the well-trodden path of traditional instruction. Community settings also played a decisive role in stimulating the emergence of the Pet Project by involving educators in a communitywide problem-solving effort.

What deserves emphasis here is that an undertaking of this kind requires considerable interaction and cooperation among community members, principals, teachers, and students. Such cooperation is best achieved when people interact in small units that allow for direct communication with one another so that they can plan together and assume responsibility for implementing their own ideas.

6

How Effective
Is Group Investigation?

In Chapter 1 we discussed the rationale for Group Investigation as developed in the works of outstanding philosophers and psychologists. In subsequent chapters we described how Group Investigation can be implemented. Educators are understandably curious to know how Group Investigation actually affects students. Can we support the claim that Group Investigation's impact on students differs from that of other forms of teaching and learning? In particular, does school learning with the Group Investigation method affect students differently than traditional whole-class instruction? It is important to know whether our claims and assertions have a basis in reality or whether they are more in the realm of pious wishes.

A substantial amount of classroom-based research has been published on the effects of cooperative learning. We will not undertake to review here the many fascinating studies carried out by the people engaged in this research. We must refer readers to the latest publications on that subject (Cohen, 1986; Johnson, Maruyama, Johnson, Nelson, & Skon, 1981; S. Sharan, 1980, 1990a; Slavin, 1983a, 1983b). Here we will limit our discussion exclusively to studies done to evaluate the effects of Group Investigation.

Research using Group Investigation has encompassed a large number of classrooms at almost all levels of public education and a broad spectrum of subject areas. All of the experiments were conducted in real classrooms as they are typically comprised in school and over a fairly long period of time. We wanted to avoid obtaining results that were artificial in any way.

Most of these studies required several years for completion because the teachers who participated in these projects first had to become proficient in the Group Investigation method. They had taught exclusively by the whole-class method for their entire professional careers prior to their participation in the experiment on cooperative learning. In each study we conducted a series of workshops to help teachers acquire the skills they needed. The workshops were also directed at helping teachers cope with their doubts and fear of failure in using a new and very different approach to instruction.

In every project we conducted, small teams of teachers were set up in each school to provide mutual assistance for planning *what* and *how* to teach. The teams were established following the teachers' participation in the workshops. Members of each small team, usually numbering three teachers, observed one another's behavior during a lesson taught with the Group Investigation approach. Immediately after the lesson, the teachers gave one another objective feedback on what they saw and heard. These comments were based on notes they took according to a prearranged list of three or four items that directed their observation. The teachers in each team agreed upon these criteria for observation prior to the lesson. The self-help teams provided an invaluable link between the teachers' experience in the workshops and their implementation of Group Investigation in their classrooms (S. Sharan et al., 1984; S. Sharan & Hertz-Lazarowitz, 1982). Examples of the principles and design of workshops for training teachers in the Group Investigation method, as well as details on the conduct of teacher self-help teams, appear in Chapter 7.

Before proceeding to the results of classroom research, we wish to point out that a very large number of classrooms in many countries are now populated by children from a wide range of nationalities and ethnic groups. Fewer and fewer classrooms in public education are ethnically homogeneous, as they were several decades ago. Since their inception, cooperative learning methods have been directed at creating positive conditions for effective instruction and social integration in the ethnically heterogeneous classroom. Classroom learning conducted with cooperative small groups of students provides a social setting conducive to the development of friendly relationships among students from different ethnic and social groups. These small groups also make possible constructive and productive interaction among group members in terms of achieving the goals of school learning. By affording all participants in the group an opportunity to contribute to the group's progress, cooperative learning methods create conditions that help students acquire status and acceptance in their groups. In the following sections of this chapter, we examine the effects of the Group Investigation method on students in the heterogeneous classroom. For information regarding the effects of other cooperative learning methods in the heterogeneous classroom setting, we refer the reader to other sources (Cohen, 1986; S. Sharan, 1990a, 1990b; Slavin, 1983a, 1990).

The studies described here were performed in Israel. A few details about Israel's population are necessary to understand the results we report in this chapter. Israel's Jewish population consists of two main ethnic groups: Those who came from the countries of the Middle East, and those who came from Western countries, including Europe and North and South America. A large percentage of the people of lower socioeconomic status in Israel are from Middle Eastern ethnic background.

ACADEMIC ACHIEVEMENT

Five of the studies assessed student achievement. Students in elementary (grades 4–8) and secondary schools (grades 7, 8, and 10) took achievement tests both before and after they had studied for months in classrooms conducted with the Group Investigation method. In most cases, these tests contained different levels and kinds of questions, requiring students not only to provide information but also to interpret and apply information to new problems and situations.

In order to better understand the results of our study, we typically divided the questions on the achievement tests into two categories: those that invited either low- or high-level thinking. This classification of the questions was made on the basis of teachers' judgments. The progress in student achievement from the pretest to the post-test in the Group Investigation classes matched, or was significantly higher than, the progress of their schoolmates in classes conducted with the traditional whole-class method. Invariably, students from the Group Investigation classes responded in a superior way to questions assessing the kind of thinking that required analysis and application of knowledge to new problems. In only one study was their knowledge of basic information about the topic, as reflected on the tests, inferior to that of students from the traditionally taught classes (S. Sharan et al., 1984). Moreover, these results of student achievement were obtained in a range of subjects, including social studies, arithmetic, reading comprehension, history, geography, literature, and biology (Lazarowitz & Karsenty, 1990; S. Sharan et al., 1984;

S. Sharan et al., 1980; S. Sharan & Shachar, 1988; S. Sharan & Shaulov, 1990).

Of particular interest are the findings from the study by S. Sharan & Shachar (1988) that analyzed pupils' spoken language during discussions held toward the conclusion of one extensive experiment. Two multiethnic groups of six pupils each were selected from 11 classrooms (eighth grade) in the same junior high school, 6 classes taught for 6 months prior to the discussions with the Group Investigation method and 5 with the traditional whole-class approach. Each of the 22 groups held two discussions of 15 minutes each, one on geography and one on history. All of the discussions were recorded on videotape and carefully analyzed by objective judges.

The data revealed that pupils from both the lower-class Middle Eastern background (often considered to be culturally deprived, with poor language ability) and the middle-class Western ethnic groups used more words per turn of speech (each time they talked) than did their ethnic peers from the classes in the same school taught with the whole-class method. Moreover, the Middle Eastern children who studied in the Group Investigation classes used as many words each time they spoke during the discussion as did the middle-class children from the classrooms conducted with the whole-class method. Finally, students from Western background generally dominated the discussions in the groups selected from the classes taught with the whole-class method.

On the other hand, in the discussion groups from the Group Investigation classes, children from both Middle Eastern and Western ethnic groups participated with equal frequency in the discussion. In the classes taught with the whole-class method, the students from the Western group took an average of 45 turns per student during the half-hour discussion, while students with a Middle Eastern background took only an average of 26 turns per student. Findings about the groups who had studied in the Group Investigation classes were very different. The Western students from these classes spoke an average of 38 times during the discussion, and the Middle Eastern students took an average of 36 turns per student during the same amount of time. Clearly, the Group Investigation approach succeeded in correcting an imbalance in the participation of children from the two ethnic groups. Those from more privileged Western backgrounds no longer dominated the groups' work as they had heretofore. Many teachers have found this imbalance to be typical of multiethnic classrooms in different parts of the world (Cohen, 1984; S. Sharan, 1980; S. Sharan & Rich, 1984; S. Sharan & Shachar, 1988).

We see, therefore, that lower-class children from a lower-status ethnic group (Middle Eastern) can and will participate in discussions about academic subjects no differently than their middle-class (Western) peers when they know that they have an equal chance to express themselves. Students must be confident that their classmates will listen to them. In cooperative learning classes, they understand that they do not have to recite in front of the entire class. Instead, they talk in a natural fashion to a small group of fellow students, all of whom have learned to cooperate with one another. In such conditions, the middle-class students no longer dominate the discussion, and everyone joins in. In this latter case, the students' social-class background affects their behavior, their speech, and their thinking about the subject matter far less than it does in the traditional classroom.

INTRINSIC MOTIVATION

We also wished to learn if participation in classroom learning conducted with the Group Investigation method enhanced the students' interest in what they were studying. We were *not* directly concerned with studying their productivity per se, namely their achievement, which is most frequently used as a measure of whether students are motivated or not. From our perspective, the central question was whether the students displayed greater involvement in the process of learning and were more interested in the substance of what they were doing when they studied in Group Investigation classes compared to fellow students taught with the whole-class method. Although much has been written about cooperative learning and its effects on motivation (Johnson & Johnson, 1985; Slavin, 1983a, 1983b, 1987), there is very little direct evidence available from research on the actual effects of cooperative learning in general, and of the Group Investigation method in particular, on children's motivation to learn.

The one study relevant here was conducted in 17 classrooms (553 students) at the sixth-grade level in four elementary schools (S. Sharan & Shaulov, 1990). All of the sixth-grade teachers in these schools (a total of 49 teachers, 28 in the cooperative learning classes and 21 in the traditionally taught classes) participated in the study, which took place over the course of two academic years. During the first year, the teachers attended workshops on Group Investigation. During the second year, we carried out all of the evaluations needed to assess the students' achievement and motivation to learn. Ten classes studied arithmetic, Bible, and language arts (reading comprehension) with the Group Investigation method, while seven classes continued to study these same topics with the whole-class method.

The complete results from this study are reported elsewhere (S. Sharan & Shaulov, 1990). Here we will focus on the topic of students' motivation to learn and how it was affected by the Group Investigation method. The main technique used in this study to find out if there were differences in the extent to which students from different classrooms became interested and involved in their studies was to give them a simple choice. When the lesson was over, the students were given the opportunity to stay in the room and continue working on their study project, or they could go outside and play on the playground for 20 minutes. That was the choice to be made. No other explanations or reasons were given to the students. The teacher and one person on the research team carefully and unobtrusively wrote down the names of the children who stayed in the room and those who left. This technique was repeated for each of the three subject classes at the beginning of the academic year and once again at the end of the year. The student body of the 10 Group Investigation classes and the 7 traditional classes remained the same in all of the three subjects. Hence each class was given a total of six opportunities to make this choice. In our judgment, deciding to stay in the room and continue one's studies was an indication of how much a student was interested in his or her studies. No rewards of any kind were offered or promised to the students for remaining in the room, nor was any comment of any kind made to anyone afterwards, whether they went outside or stayed in the room.

In addition to this method for evaluating the students' motivation, we were able to use information routinely recorded by teachers about their students. All teachers recorded their evaluation of the students' willingness to invest effort in preparing homework and the extent to which students participated actively in classroom discussions about academic material. These latter two measures also reflected students' motivation to learn, albeit in a somewhat less direct and self-evident manner. Thus three sources of information about each student were used: (1) the student's decision to persevere at a study task instead of playing outside, (2) teachers' evaluation of the extent to which the student invested effort in homework, and (3) teachers' evaluation of the student's classroom participation. The evaluations of four teachers (homeroom, arithmetic, Bible, and language) were collected for each student, so that these evaluations did not reflect the opinion of one teacher alone for any given student.

The analysis of these data showed that the students' willingness to stay in the room and continue working on academic subject matter was the single most effective indicator of students' academic achievement as reflected in their school grades for both years of this study, that is, when the students were in the fifth and sixth grades. The other two measures derived from the teachers added weight to the prediction that could be made as to the students' level of achievement. Moreover, the students' motivation to learn was found to be a significant factor leading to academic achievement. Of course, teachers have known that for a long time, but it is not often found in controlled research studies.

Finally, there were significant changes in the level of motivation over the course of the year among students in classes taught with different instructional methods. Students in all classes began the year at approximately the same level of motivation on all three measures. Those from the Group Investigation classes revealed a large increase in their motivation to learn over the course of the year. This was in contrast to the students who studied with the whole-class method, who did not display any increase at all in their level of motivation. Interestingly enough, the group taught with the whole-class method did not reveal any decline in their motivation, which speaks well for the teachers who participated in this project. A decrease in student motivation over the course of the year in school is not uncommon in our schools. In sum, the evidence available at this time shows that Group Investigation can enhance students' intrinsic motivation to learn.

SOCIAL INTERACTION

Interaction between classmates who studied together with the Group Investigation method has been evaluated from several points of view. Above and beyond the topic of academic achievement, the most important questions that educators ask themselves about the effects of cooperative learning on their students are: Do the students really learn to cooperate, maintain friendly relations, and help one another? Do students from different ethnic groups in the so-called heterogeneous classroom relate to one another more positively in the cooperative classroom than they did before? In particular, how are the less advantaged students affected by cooperative learning in terms of their social relations with their peers?

Research on cooperative learning has always taken a deep interest in the study of these questions, and the results of this extensive work have been reported by many investigators (Cohen, 1986; Cohen, Lotan, & Catanzarite, 1990; Johnson & Johnson, 1987; Johnson, Johnson, & Maruyama, 1983; Miller & Harrington, 1990; S. Sharan, 1990a, 1990b; Slavin, 1983a, 1990). Once again, we will concentrate exclusively on results from studies done with the Group Investigation method. Except for one notable exception to be discussed later, the social relations among students in the Group Investigation classes were compared to those among students who studied in classes taught with the whole-class method.

Like all societies, large or small, classroom life poses many social challenges for students throughout their years in school. What we wish to stress here is that the manner in which teachers organize and conduct classroom learning affects students' social relationships in different ways. Classrooms are not socially neutral places. Many teachers ignore the social dimensions of classroom teaching and concentrate exclusively on study tasks. Yet, whatever be teachers' choice of instructional method, it will exert its effects on student relationships. In turn, these relationships will exert their critical influences on students' attitudes toward school and on the way they pursue the process of learning (Schmuck & Schmuck, 1988).

Cooperative learning arranges for students to maintain a great deal more interpersonal contact with their classmates than is possible under conditions of whole-class instruction. Much of this contact is for the purpose of having students help one another study subject matter in many ways. That alone contributes to closer relationships among students who attend school every day in company with the same people. Moreover, there is no doubt that, by comparison to the Group Investigation method, whole-class instruction stimulates a great deal of competition among students and little cooperation. Group Investigation, on the other hand, does in fact promote cooperation and mutual assistance among pupils. It has been shown, too, that these helpful relations among students, fostered by their experience in cooperative classrooms, affect their relationships outside of their classrooms as well, when the teacher is not present to observe them (Hertz-Lazarowitz, S. Sharan, & Steinberg, 1980; S. Sharan, 1990b; S. Sharan et al., 1984).

Important, too, is the finding from research that this kind of positive interaction with classmates occurs between students from different ethnic groups as well as among those from the same group.

Competition is known to create emotional distance, even animosity, between people. This is true especially when they are from different cultural groups and might encounter obstacles in establishing positive relations with people from other groups or in accepting, or being accepted by, members of other groups. Teachers of ethnically heterogeneous classrooms would be ill advised to employ teaching methods that highlight the ability of some students to consistently win out over other students. Competition invariably creates losers, and these turn out most frequently to be students from lower-class ethnic groups. This undesirable situation is almost inevitable under conditions of whole-class teaching. But it can be effectively avoided. Positive peer relationships can be promoted by having students cooperate in the process of learning in the manner suggested by the Group Investigation method. The message appears repeatedly in reports about research on the Group Investigation method: It has many positive effects on the interaction and relationships between students from different ethnic groups in heterogeneous classrooms (Cohen, 1984; Cohen et al., 1990; S. Sharan, 1990b; S. Sharan et al., 1984; S. Sharan & Rich, 1984; S. Sharan & Shachar, 1988).

TEACHERS' STYLE OF TALKING WHILE TEACHING

Students in most schools must listen to teachers talk several hours each day. No doubt the way teachers talk, including the manner in which they verbally present academic subject matter, has important consequences for children's education. The Group Investigation method seems to have a profound effect on teachers' manner of speaking in the classroom by comparison with the manner of their speech in traditionally taught classes. Twenty-two teachers who taught grades 1–6 were tape-recorded three times during the first semester of the year when they taught their classes with the whole-class approach (Hertz-Lazarowitz & Shachar, 1990). Their verbal behavior was tape-recorded again three times during the second semester of the same year when they conducted their classes with the Group Investigation method. In this fashion, it was possible to compare the speech of each teacher to herself when using two completely different approaches to classroom teaching. Readers interested in the way the teachers' speech was analyzed can consult the original publication of this study.

The study informs us that teachers' speech differs considerably in classrooms taught with the different methods. Teachers do not talk to their students the same way regardless of how the class is organized and of how instruction proceeds. These factors have a far-reaching effect on the entire verbal behavior of teachers in the classroom. The fact that, in the study we are discussing, the same teachers taught in both the Group Investigation and in the traditional classrooms shows that the differences in teachers' talk derive from their styles of teaching, not from their personalities.

In the classes taught with the whole-class method, the teachers spoke in a very formal manner. They lectured, gave instructions, asked short questions, enforced collective discipline, and expressed general praise to the class not directed at specific students. By contrast, in the Group Investigation classes, the teachers spoke in a distinctly informal manner. They encouraged students to display initiative, helped students pursue their study tasks, made it easier for students to communicate directly with one another, gave students feedback on their work, and praised individual students for specific acts. It seems reasonable to conclude that the Group Investigation approach to classroom teaching creates conditions for more personal, accepting, and constructive verbal communication between teachers and students than the traditional whole-class form of instruction. These latter results are consistent with the finding from another study that showed that teachers in Group Investigation classes expressed much less need to control the class and the children's behavior than did teachers in classrooms taught with the whole-class method (Sharan & Hertz-Lazarowitz, 1982).

Tighter discipline and control, more formalistic speech, greater emotional distance between the teacher and students, even less personal support for students, little direct interaction among the students for purposes of learning, and a fundamentally extrinsic form of motivation with all of its implications—these and other characteristics have been found in many classrooms conducted with the whole-class method. These characteristics need to be changed, and they do, in fact, become significantly reduced in importance in classes taught with the Group Investigation approach. Implementing the Group Investigation method implies change in many features of classroom teaching and learning. Taken together, these changes result in discernible improvement in the entire atmosphere prevailing in the classroom. Teachers feel more positive and enthusiastic about their work, and they report that many more students become involved in active study. On their part, the students are able to derive far greater pleasure, benefit, and personal meaning from their classroom experience.

7

Preparing Teachers
for Group Investigation

Readers of this book surely appreciate that Group Investigation differs considerably in theory and practice from traditional whole-class instruction. Prospective teachers of Group Investigation have to acquire skills for organizing the classroom and facilitating the implementation of this method. They also must acquire skills for analyzing and evaluating its implementation. The preceding chapters describe how to prepare a class for Group Investigation and how to carry it out stage by stage, step by step. However, effective implementation of this method, as indeed of any teaching method, calls for more than the application of a series of distinct acts. In order to integrate the various aspects of Group Investigation, we recommend that teachers actually experience them.

The two training programs represented in this chapter are based on the experiential learning model (Kolb & Fry, 1975). These programs enable teachers to learn the structure and process of Group Investigation while carrying it out. They are particularly suited to adult learners of different ages, backgrounds, and interests (Kolb & Lewis, 1986; Y. Sharan & S. Sharan, 1987). Both programs construct a setting that combines the four components of the model: experience, reflection, conceptualization, and planning, in which teachers simulate a Group Investigation classroom. In this simulated setting, teachers can encounter the many personal and professional implications of this model of teaching. This applies to Program A, for teachers less familiar with cooperative learning, as well as to Program B, for teachers familiar with cooperative learning. We conclude the chapter with guidelines for establishing teacher self-help teams, which carry on the process begun in these training workshops.

THE TRAINING PROGRAMS

Goals

Preparing for Implementation.   The main goal of the two training programs presented in this chapter is to prepare teachers to implement Group Investigation. The participating teachers carry out each stage of Group Investigation and thus experience each one of its components. This entails planning their inquiry cooperatively, exchanging ideas and information with one another, seeking information and ideas from a variety of sources, seeing one another as potential sources of knowledge, and becoming active participants in the learning process.

In order to stimulate the students to investigate topics that they find challenging and intriguing, teachers take on many roles: class manager, consultant, evaluator, group facilitator, and individual supporter. They do not present themselves as the sole source of information about the topic to be investigated. "The emphasis instead, is on encouraging students to discover and pool their expertise, and it is the teacher's adoption of such an emphasis that enables individual learners within the group to contribute meaningfully to the ongoing inquiry" (Wells et al., 1990, p. 99). Throughout the training program the trainer models these roles and strives to create a climate that fosters this stance.

Preparing for Uncertainty.   Group Investigation does not involve production-type tasks, when every element is specifiable and where outcomes are largely preplanned. The interaction among individual learners in the group cannot be entirely predicted or controlled by the teacher. Therefore the two training programs presented here strive to have teachers accommodate to varying degrees of uncertainty as to what their students will contribute and produce when they conduct a Group Investigation project.

Facilitating cooperative planning and inquiry is a challenge teachers face anew with each class, since each class presents a new situation with new factors to be considered. Group Investigation will most likely be implemented in a different way in each class. That is not to say that teachers must begin from scratch with each new class. They will certainly rely on their knowledge of the general structure and process of Group Investigation, but they must also be able to adapt the stages and steps of the model to the specific needs of each class. Therefore, when preparing teachers to carry out Group Investigation, we do not stipulate a specific set of rules to be reproduced in a routine fashion. Teachers who study Group Investigation will not receive a list of "recipes" that have predetermined outcomes.

Another probable cause for uncertainty is the students' reactions to the process of inquiry. Teachers may wonder whether students will ask enough questions, "cover the material," understand the main point of what they read, and know how to summarize the material. In all likelihood, the students will share the feeling of uncertainty about the process and outcomes of Group Investigation, especially the first time they carry it out. The four components of the experiential learning model (experience, reflection, conceptualization, and planning) prepare teachers for organizing and conducting Group Investigation competently so that they can enable their students to do the same.

The Model

Experience and Reflection.   The two training programs presented here provide teachers with an opportunity to create and experience a full Group Investigation project. Instead of learning *about* this method, they learn mainly by doing it, with the addition of systematic reflection about what they did. Participants share their thoughts, satisfactions, and doubts about the process of Group Investigation. They also heighten their awareness of their own strengths and weaknesses as investigators and as facilitators of investigation.

During the reflective discussions held during each workshop, teachers bring past teaching experience to bear on the new experience of conducting a Group Investigation. They help one another articulate the similarities and differences between their old and new experiences of teaching. To the extent that conducting Group Investigation is new for participants, the workshop provides a situation that does not fit their accustomed routine or categories of "knowing-in-action" (Schön, 1987). Teachers are encouraged to rethink many of their assumptions about teaching and learning—even about cooperative learning. By establishing the norm of reflection in the training workshop, the trainer encourages constant evaluation of what is being learned.

Throughout the workshops the trainer is also engaged in the process of balancing what he or she knows about preparing teachers for Group Investigation with the specific reactions of the teachers in the present setting. For the trainer, just as for the prospective teacher of Group Investigation, there is no one predictable outcome of the recommended sequence of activities. Trainers must respond to the teachers' particular reactions to the structure and process of Group Investigation and modify their plans accordingly. For example, some principles of Group Investigation may require more emphasis than planned; some suggested activities may be discarded; or more time may have to be devoted to planning implementation or to developing communication skills. When the trainer modifies any aspect of the original plan, he or she should explain to the teachers what led to that decision. Thus the trainer models "reflection-in-action" (Schön, 1987) and the flexibility that underlie the practice of Group Investigation. Everybody involved is constantly learning.

Conceptualizing and Planning. The experiential learning model also develops the teachers' conceptual framework and lends order to their observations and reflections about their experience. When they summarize what they have learned from carrying out the stages of Group Investigation, teachers organize their experiences according to general principles about the structure and process of this method. These principles then serve as a basis for decisions about how to plan the implementation of Group Investigation in their classroom.

Teachers in the two sets of workshops are free to learn in a setting relatively low in risk, with access to the trainer as well as one another for support and for information. Teachers bring to this setting "generic competencies for communication, experimentation and imitation on which they can build" (Schön, 1987, p. 118), through dialogue with one another and with the trainer, in order to learn Group Investigation.

Each of the two staff development programs consists of five sessions. The average length of a workshop session is approximately three hours. However, sessions can differ in the amount of time needed to complete the recommended activities. Trainers should use their judgment and add any introductory, team-building activities they consider appropriate. Ideally, each session should allow the participants as much time as they need to acquire competence and confidence in conducting Group Investigation.

————————————— **Training Program A** —————————————

For Teachers Less Familiar with
Cooperative Learning

SESSION I: COOPERATIVE PLANNING

The trainer begins this session with an explanation of the experiential nature of the method in which the workshop will be conducted and a short description of cooperative planning.

Activity 1: Create a Group Poster

This is *one* of a pool of games and exercises that illustrate different ways of organizing groups and cooperative planning tasks as well as provide practice in a wide range of communication skills (Cohen, 1986; Graves & Graves, 1990; Kagan, 1989; Schmuck & Runkel, 1985; Schmuck & Schmuck, 1988; Stanford & Stanford, 1969). The trainer may choose to conduct more than one of these activities, based on the teachers' needs.

Objectives:
Plan and carry out a cooperative planning activity.
Demonstrate any previous knowledge of cooperative learning.
Create an environment that reflects individual personalities and
group choices.

Materials:
Poster board, magazines, markers, tape, paste, scissors for each
group.

Method:
Divide randomly into groups of five.
Each group is instructed to decide together on a poster.
Each group plans together how to carry out the assignment.
Each group creates its poster.
Groups present their posters and explain their meaning.
All posters are hung on the wall.

Activity 2: Debrief the Process

Objective:

Reflect upon personal and general significance of the previous activity.

Method:

Each group reviews how it organized its work and the interaction that took place in the group.

Each group chooses a representative to report to the class.

The instructor asks for one group to report its findings.

Subsequent groups will be asked to highlight similarities and point out differences.

The instructor lists all findings on the board (or on newsprint) without judgment.

Some of the findings may be:

- We decided on a theme for our poster.
- At first we didn't know what to do, then we talked about it for a while and came to a decision.
- We really had to listen to each other.

Activity 3: Categorize Basic Principles

Objective:

Generalize some of the basic principles of cooperative planning in small groups.

Method:

In pairs, teachers deduce and formulate basic principles from the list of findings (from the previous activity).

Each pair compares its list with another pair.

Each quartet reports its list of principles.

The instructor leads the class as a whole in a discussion intended to reach consensus. The principles are written on a chart, to be posted.

The list of principles may include the following:

- Cooperative planning is based on communication skills.
- Groups plan and create a collective product that reflects each member's contribution.
- The planning task for a group should allow for choice.

Activity 4: Prepare a Cooperative Planning Activity

Objective:
Plan a one-period cooperative planning activity for the classroom.

Materials (optional):
Books, workbooks from subject matter of teachers' choice.

Method:
Teachers form groups of two or three according to grade level and/or subject matter.

Teachers plan an activity for their students that requires cooperative planning skills. Instructor reminds teachers to refer to posted chart of basic principles of cooperative planning as a checklist.

Instructor provides examples from various grade levels and subject matter:
- Second-grade students plan in pairs how to study the week's spelling assignment.
- Fifth-graders in dyads trace their foot outlines, then plan a few ways to figure the area of each foot (Burns, 1987).
- Sixth-grade students plan a timeline for raising money for the school band to go to the Rose Parade.
- Journalism class plans in groups how to interview, groups present suggestions to whole class, and class arrives at consensus as to the best way to conduct an interview.

Three groups combine to share and evaluate their plans, referring to the posted list of principles.

Instructor circulates among groups and gives guidance where needed.

As a form of closure, each teacher writes down what he or she learned in this session about cooperative planning. The instructor invites sharing of what was learned with the whole class.

SESSION II: CARRY OUT GROUP INVESTIGATION OF COMMUNICATION SKILLS

Communication in a learning group involves more than a few people having a casual conversation with one another. Communication is a process and a relationship. Each participant in the group must want to speak for some good reason, and the listener must want to hear for equally good reasons. Cooperative planning requires a great deal of talk among group members. How do group members acquire the skills necessary for conducting a discussion that facilitates the group's work? What is the teacher's role in developing these skills? These are the key questions that groups will investigate in this session.

In the following activities we explore the students' and the teacher's role by using the Group Investigation method. In this way teachers gain experience in carrying out a cooperative inquiry (the process) while they learn about communication skills (the content).

Activity 1: Learners Plan Their Investigation

Objective:
Experience first-hand the stages of Group Investigation.

Materials:
Sources that may be used for the research on communication:
- Excerpts from articles on communication provided by the trainer.
- List of nonacademic games and activities that promote discussion skills, provided by the trainer.
- A film or videotape of students conducting a discussion.
- Handout: Stages of Implementation of Group Investigation, (see Figure 4.1).

Method:
Trainer asks, "What do you want to know about communication skills that facilitate learning in groups?" Individuals scan the sources. Cooperative planning of the subtopics can proceed in one of three ways:
1. The trainer presents the problem to the entire class and asks, "What do you think is important to know about this problem?" Each teacher raises questions about the aspect of the problem he or she would like to investigate. The trainer writes the questions on the board. OR:
2. Teachers meet in "buzz" groups. Each person expresses his or her ideas about what to investigate. Recorders from each buzz group write down all ideas and report them to the whole class. A short class discussion results in a shared list of suggestions for subtopics to be investigated. OR:
3. Planning begins with each teacher writing down his or her suggestions. Afterwards planning continues in progressively larger groups, from pairs to quartets or even to groups of

eight. At each step group members compare their lists, eliminate repetitions, and compile a single list. This final list represents the interests of all members.

The next step is to make all the suggestions available to the whole class. This can be done by writing them all on the board or on newsprint that is hung on the walls, or by mimeographing them and distributing a copy to everyone.

After each teacher has a list of everyone's suggestions, the next step is to classify them into several categories. This step can be conducted by one of the three methods outlined above. The end product incorporates the ideas and interests of all class members, organized into categories. These categories are then presented as the subtopics for separate group investigations. Possible subtopics include:

- Which communication skills are appropriate for lower grades?
- Which communication skills are appropriate for middle grades?
- What are the various types of discussions? (brainstorming, buzz groups, problem solving, decision making, etc.)

Activity 2: Each Group Plans Its Investigation

Objective:
Groups determine the specific questions they will investigate.

Method:
Each group spends some time choosing the questions they will investigate, deciding which resources are needed to carry out its investigation and how to divide the work among themselves. Many groups find it useful to fill out a worksheet, as illustrated in Figure 7.1.

The trainer posts a copy of each group's worksheet on the wall, so as to give the whole class an overview of the investigation project as a whole and demonstrate the connection between the various subtopics.

Activity 3: Each Group Carries Out Its Investigation

Objective:
Each group carries out the plans they formulated in the previous activity.

Figure 7.1   Group Planning Form

OUR SUBTOPIC: What kinds of communication skills do groups need
                       in order to work together?

NAMES OF GROUP MEMBERS: Sally, Mark, Kemp, Helen

WHAT DO WE WANT
TO INVESTIGATE?   1.   What are the basic communication skills?
                       2.   What are the different types of discussions?
                       3.   Can we match specific communication skills
                            with specific types of group tasks?

WHAT ARE OUR
RESOURCES?   1.   Chapter on discussion skills in Sharan &
                            Sharan, *Small Group Teaching*.
                       2.   Chapter 6 in Johnson & Johnson, *Learning
                            Together and Alone*.
                       3.   Stanford & Stanford, *Learning Discussion
                            Skills Through Games*.
                       4.   ---------

HOW WILL WE
DIVIDE THE WORK?   Sally and Kemp--question 1
                       Mark and Helen--question 2
                       Whole group--question 3 (after hearing the
                       answers to 1 &2)

HOW WILL WE PRESENT OUR FINDINGS?*
We'll lead the class in two exercises: "Survival in the Desert" and "The Mystery
Game", each of which requires different type of communication. After the
exercises we'll ask the class to divide into groups and discuss which kinds of
communication skills were needed in each exercise. We'll then ask them to
share their thoughts with the whole group. Afterwards we'll ask them to plan a
few activities for their classrooms that require the same types of communication
skills.

*This item may be filled out after the investigation has yielded a few findings.

Method:

Teachers singly or in pairs gather information, analyze and evaluate the data, reach conclusions, and apply their share of new knowledge to the resolution of the group's topic that interests them most; in so doing, each contributes one part necessary to the creation of a group "whole." The work may be done during the workshop, but, if possible, teachers should meet between sessions to complete their investigation.

When individuals or pairs complete their portion of the task, the group reconvenes and members share their progress. Groups may choose to have one member record their conclusions, or each member may present a written summary of his or her findings.

At the end of this activity the trainer will ask each group to appoint a representative to a steering committee.

Activity 4: Each Group Prepares Its Final Report

Objective:

Each group decides what to report and how to make their presentation.

Method:

Presentations consist of a visual model, a written report, games, or other activities (see pp. 85–86 for guidelines for preparing a final report).

Representatives of the steering committee meet with the trainer to coordinate time schedules and to make sure that all group members are involved in the presentation. The trainer continues the role of advisor and helps the committee as needed.

SESSION III (CONTINUATION OF SESSION II)

Activity 5: Each Group Presents Its Final Report

Objectives:

Identify the various communication skills involved in Group Investigation.

Demonstrate exercises and games for developing communication skills.

Plan implementation of communication skills in classroom.

Method:

The class as a whole determines criteria for evaluating the presentations, such as:
- Did the group succeed in clearly presenting the main findings?
- Did every group member participate?
- Did the presentation actively involve the class?

Activity 6: Teachers Summarize Guidelines for Implementation

Objective:

Establish criteria for developing communication skills.

Method:

After hearing each group's report, the class meets as a "group of groups." The trainer leads the discussion to summarize those communication skills most needed for successful group work. These are listed on newsprint and posted on the wall.

The class establishes guidelines for developing communication skills in the classroom. This may be done in a classwide discussion or first in groups and then classwide. The guidelines are written on newsprint and posted on the wall. The list may include the following:
- Begin training in communication skills with nonacademic activities and games.
- Vary the training by working with the whole class or with one group at a time.
- Combine training in communication skills with content learning (e.g., discuss the merits of the Constitution as part of a listening exercise).
- Have students serve as observers during group discussions.
- Teachers must model effective communication skills by listening patiently, checking for understanding, and so forth.

Activity 7: Teachers Plan Implementation

Objective:

Teachers plan how to develop communication skills in their classroom.

Method:

Teachers form groups by grade level and/or subject matter and prepare an outline for developing communication skills in their classrooms.

Teachers should be reminded to base their planning on the criteria established in activity 6 in this session. For instance:
- Conduct whole-class discussion in a particular content area with the teacher modeling the following: listening, encouraging participation, paraphrasing, and so forth.
- Divide the whole class into buzz groups that conduct a preliminary discussion in preparation for classwide clarification of an issue.
- Conduct discussion with one small group, while the rest of the class does something else.

SESSION IV: GENERALIZE ABOUT GROUP INVESTIGATION

Activity 1: Reflection

Objective:
Reflect on the experience of conducting a group investigation.

Method:
Teachers discuss their answers to these questions:
- How was the investigation carried out? (review stages of Group Investigation)
- What kind of learning took place at each stage?
- What problems arose during each stage? What ways can we suggest for dealing with these problems?

The discussion proceeds in one of three ways:
1. Instructor writes each stage of Group Investigation on a separate sheet of newsprint and hangs it on the wall. Each group discusses the above questions and sends a representative to write the group findings on the appropriate sheet. Instructor leads whole class in summarizing discussion. OR:
2. Instructor writes each stage of Group Investigation on a separate sheet of newsprint and hangs it on the wall. Each group chooses to analyze one or two stages of Group Investigation. A representative of each group writes its findings on the appropriate sheet. Instructor leads class discussion and summarizes issues under appropriate heading. OR:
3. Each group discusses the above three questions and prepares a written summary. A representative of each group then participates in a panel. Each representative presents his

or her group's findings. The trainer leads the panel in a summary discussion.

Activity 2: Plan Outline of Group Investigation

Objective:
Plan implementation of Group Investigation in the classroom.

Materials:
Content area material (brought by teachers).
Chapter 4 of this book.
Summary of types of learning in Group Investigation from activity 1 in this session.

Method:
Form groups according to grade level (no more than four in a group).
Decide on content area and timeframe of lesson or lessons.
Write the outline and make copies for other groups.

SESSION V: PRESENT GROUP INVESTIGATION OUTLINES

Activity 1: Discuss How to Evaluate Presentations

Objective:
Determine criteria for evaluating presentations.

Method:
Teachers discuss criteria for evaluating presentations. For instance: Did all the teachers take part in planning? Did the group use its resources well? Did their outline for Group Investigation include the basic features of this method?

Activity 2: Presentations

Objective:
Present and evaluate outlines.

Method:
Each group presents its outline; all groups participate in evaluation of the presentation, according to criteria agreed upon in activity 1 in this session.

Activity 3: Wrap-up

Objective:
Summarize what was learned in the workshops.

Method:
Suggested questions for discussion (classwide or in groups):
- What are the advantages of Group Investigation?
- What are the problems of Group Investigation?
- When is it best to conduct Group Investigation in a class?
- What more do we need to know in order to master Group Investigation? How can we continue learning what is needed?

If possible, summarize how the Group Investigation strategy can be combined with other cooperative learning methods.

———————— Training Program B ————————
For Teachers with Prior Experience
in Cooperative Learning

The sessions in this program parallel the six stages of Group Investigation.

SESSION I: ORGANIZATION STAGE

Four Structural Dimensions of the Classroom.   (This script is to be used as a resource for the trainer.)

Classroom learning through cooperative group investigation has its sources in philosophical and psychological writings of the past 75 years. First among the prominent forebears of this educational orientation was John Dewey. Dewey viewed cooperation in the classroom as a prerequisite for dealing with the complex problems of life in a democracy. The classroom is a cooperative enterprise where teacher and pupils build the learning process on mutual planning, based on their respective experiences, capacities, and needs. Learners are active participants in all aspects of school life, making choices and decisions that determine the goals toward which they work. The group, whether large or small, affords the social vehicle for developing this process. Group planning is the method for ensuring maximum pupil involvement.

The main features of Group Investigation are evident in the four structural dimensions of the classroom. These dimensions are *the organizational features of the classroom, the design of the learning task, the pupils' behavior, and the teacher's behavior* (Sharan & Hertz-Lazarowitz, 1980; Hertz-Lazarowitz & Davidson, 1990).

1. *The organizational features of the classroom.* The class is divided into small groups numbering from two to six students. The groups study a specific topic for a specified period of time. Usually the various groups study different aspects of the same general topic; sometimes they work on identical subject matter. The teacher suggests the general topic based upon the planned curriculum. Each student participates in the formulation of subtopics and joins a group that will investigate the subtopic of his or her choice. Each group plans the specific content and method of study, carries out its study

plan, and prepares and presents to the entire class some form of report on its procedures, sources, and findings.

2. *The learning task* is a multifaceted problem with a variety of solutions, perspectives, and sources. This allows for discussion, perspective taking, independent judgment, and evaluation of findings. Group members plan cooperatively the different aspects of the task: what they will study, what their sources will be, and how they will divide the work among themselves. Group members work individually or in pairs on different aspects of the task. All members participate in constructing the comprehensive group product. There is constant coordination among group members during the various stages of their work.

3. *The pupils' behavior* in Group Investigation consists of planning cooperatively and coordinating with their groupmates what and how they will study. Their investigation will lead them to a variety of sources that they will evaluate, analyze in discussion, and integrate with each other. Students must communicate effectively with one another. Therefore Group Investigation is based on cooperative interaction skills (such as listening, sharing, and exchanging ideas) that students have developed in previous experience with cooperative learning.

4. *The teacher's behavior* in Group Investigation is markedly different from the traditional role. The teacher circulates among the groups, checks that they are managing their work, and helps out with any difficulties they encounter in group interaction and in performing the specific tasks related to the learning project. It is the teacher's responsibility to create a learning environment that supports curiosity, self-directed inquiry, and student decision making.

The workshops will follow the four stages of the experiential model of learning: experience, reflection, conceptualization, and planning (Kolb & Fry, 1975).

Activity 1: Generate Questions

Objectives:
Teachers generate questions about Group Investigation.

Method:
Teachers carry out an exploratory activity. They simulate a situation that requires inquiry, such as:
- How do we go about planning a move to a new city?
- How do we go about planning the development of a city park?

- How do we investigate the skills and knowledge necessary to carry out Group Investigation in our classrooms?

(All groups may choose the same activity or one of the three). The trainer asks each group to reflect on the exploratory activity by addressing these questions:

- How did you carry out this activity?
- What steps did you go through?

The answers to these questions are listed on newsprint or on the board. The trainer summarizes them and points out the connection to the stages of implementation of Group Investigation. One group may offer the following observations:

- We discussed our ideas of what the "new city" was like. We thought of different ways of finding out what it would be like.
- We listed all the things we might want to take with us.
- We listed the various ways of moving and what would be the advantages of each one.
- We decided that after "moving" we would prepare a pamphlet with guidelines for future newcomers to this city.

Activity 2: Identify Stages of Group Investigation

Objective:
Identify stages of Group Investigation.

Materials:
Handout of list of stages of Group Investigation (see Figure 4.1).

Method:
Teachers read handout and clarify any questions about the stages of implementation.

Activity 3: Cooperative Planning

Objective:
Together teachers generate questions about what they want to know about Group Investigation.

Method:
This activity can proceed in one of three ways:
1. The trainer presents the problem to the entire class and asks, "What do you want to know about Group Investiga-

tion?" Each teacher raises questions about the aspect of the issue he or she would like to investigate. OR:

2. Teachers meet in buzz groups in which each person expresses his or her ideas about what to investigate. Recorders from each buzz group write down each idea and then report them to the whole class. A short class discussion results in a shared list of suggestions for subtopics to be investigated. OR:

3. Planning begins with each teacher writing down his or her suggestions. Afterwards planning continues in progressively larger groups, from pairs to quartets or even to groups of eight. At each step group members compare their lists, eliminate repetitions, and compile a single list. This final list represents the interest of all members.

Activity 4: Classify Questions into Subtopics

Objective:
Teachers sort their questions into categories.

Method:
All the suggestions are made available to the whole class. This can be done by writing them on the board or on newsprint that is hung on the walls, or by mimeographing them and distributing a copy to each teacher.

After each teacher has a list of everyone's suggestions, the next step is to classify them into several categories. The end product incorporates the ideas and interests of all class members, sorted into categories, which are then presented as the subtopics for Group Investigation.

Participation in this stage enables teachers to express their individual interests and to exchange ideas and opinions with their classmates.

The final list of subtopics incorporates each person's contribution to the classwide effort.

Activity 5: Reflection

Objective:
Teachers reflect on the personal and professional significance of this session.

Method:
>   The trainer asks teachers to discuss these questions:
>   - What happened?
>   - What was the learner's role?
>   - What was the trainer's role?
>
>   The trainer records the observations on two separate charts, one for teacher's role and one for learner's role, and adds to them during each subsequent session.

SESSION II: GROUPS PLAN THEIR INVESTIGATIONS

Activity 1: List Subtopics

Objective:
>   Form groups on the basis of choice of subtopic.

Method:
>   The subtopics listed during session 1 are written on the board. Every participant signs up for the subtopic he or she wants to investigate. The trainer may see fit to limit group size to five. It is quite acceptable for two or more groups to study the same subtopic. If there is one subtopic that nobody chooses, then the class will be asked to decide what to do with that subtopic.

Activity 2: Groups Plan Investigation

Objective:
>   Plan what to study and how to proceed.

Method:
>   After joining the research groups of their choice, participants turn their attention to the subtopic of their choice. At this stage group members determine the aspect of the subtopic each one of them (singly or in pairs) will investigate. In effect, each group has to decide how to proceed and what resources they will need to carry out their investigation. Each group must formulate a researchable problem and plan its course of action. Many groups find it useful to fill out a "worksheet" (illustrated in Figure 4.2) that states the questions relevant to this planning stage.

A copy of each group's worksheet is posted in order to present graphic evidence that the class is a "group of groups": Each individual member contributes to the small group's investigation, and each group contributes to the whole class's study of the larger unit.

Each group cooperates in formulating a plan to carry out its investigation on its subtopics by specifying:
- What do they want to investigate?
- What are their resources?
- How will they divide the work among themselves?

Some examples of possible subtopics are:
- How can we get students to formulate appropriate questions?
- What are the communication skills students need in order to investigate in a group?
- What are some prior activities that a teacher can conduct in the classroom to prepare students for Group Investigation?
- How do you evaluate Group Investigation?
- What is the teacher's role in the cooperative learning classroom?
- Are all content areas appropriate for Group Investigation?

Activity 3: Reflection

Objective:
Teachers reflect on the personal and professional significance of this session.

Method:
The trainer asks teachers to discuss their questions:
- What happened?
- What was the learner's role?
- What was the trainer's role?

The trainer records the observations on two separate charts, one for teacher's role and one for learner's role, and adds to them during each subsequent session.

SESSION III: GROUPS COMPLETE THEIR INVESTIGATIONS AND PLAN THEIR PRESENTATION

In this session Stages III and IV are compressed into one. In the classroom each stage is conducted separately.

Activity 1: **Complete the Investigation**

Objectives:
>   Gather information, analyze the data, and reach conclusions; exchange, discuss, clarify, and synthesize ideas.

Method:
>   Participants, singly or in pairs, gather information, analyze and evaluate the data, reach conclusions, and apply their share of new knowledge to the resolution of the group's research problem. Each participant investigates that aspect of the group subtopic that interests him or her most, and in so doing contributes one part necessary to create a group product.

Activity 2: **Plan the Report**

Objectives:
>   Determine the essential message of the findings.
>   Plan what to report and how to present the report.

Method:
>   Each group decides what the group will report and how it will make its presentation. Participants can be encouraged to present factual material on a poster or handout. They should also plan an activity that actively involves the class. For example, the group that is investigating introductory activities to cooperative planning might lead the class in several appropriate exercises. Another group, investigating methods of evaluation, might hand out a sample questionnaire to the class by which they evaluate the whole workshop.

Activity 3: **Reflection**

Objective:
>   Teachers reflect on the personal and professional significance of this session.

Method:
>   The trainer asks teachers to discuss these questions:
>   • What happened?
>   • What was the learner's role?

• What was the trainer's role?

Add new observations to those listed in previous sessions.

SESSION IV: GROUPS PRESENT THEIR FINAL REPORTS

Activity 1: Evaluating Presentations

Objective:

Determine criteria for evaluation of presentations.

Method:

The class as a whole determines criteria for evaluating the presentations, such as:

• Were the findings presented clearly?

• Did every group member participate?

• Did the presentation actively involve the "audience"?

Activity 2: Presentation

Objectives:

Emphasize the main ideas and conclusions of the investigation.

Each group presents its specific contribution to class's investigation.

Method:

Each group takes a turn presenting the final "report," by teaching or demonstrating its findings to the other groups.

The "audience" evaluates each presentation according to the criteria established in activity 1 in this session.

Activity 3: Reflection

Objective:

Summarize personal and professional learning in Sessions I–IV.

Method:

The trainer conducts a classwide summary of the experience of conducting a Group Investigation. Questions to facilitate the discussion (classwide or in groups) may be:

• What kind of learning took place at each step?

- What problems arose during each stage?
- What ways can we suggest for dealing with these problems?

SESSION V: TEACHERS PLAN IMPLEMENTATION FOR THE CLASSROOM

Activity 1: Teachers Plan a Group Investigation Project

Objective:

Plan a Group Investigation project for the classroom.

Method:

Teachers group according to grade level and/or subject matter. The teachers in each group begin by identifying one or more general problems in their chosen content area that lend themselves to genuine investigation. Then they determine the general topic for investigation. This topic should be formulated as a question. For example, the general topic "The Civil War" might be phrased as "What were the causes of the Civil War?" or "How did the South change as a result of the Civil War?" Instead of presenting the general topic "Exploring Space," ask the class "What are the possible developments in space exploration in the next ten years?" or "What has space exploration achieved?" The planning of the class project can proceed in one of two ways: The group works as a whole, or members divide the task among themselves in any way they see fit.

Activity 2: Groups Share Their Plans

Objectives:

Evaluate the process of planning a Group Investigation project. Share plans with all participants.

Method:

The trainer summarizes those stages in teacher planning that were easy and those that were more difficult. The whole class discusses ways of combining Group Investigation with other cooperative learning strategies. The trainer suggests further reading and encourages teachers to continue working together in self-help teams. The planning sheet illustrated in Figure 7.2 may be helpful. Each group's plan is photocopied and distributed to all participants.

TEACHER SELF-HELP TEAMS FOR IMPLEMENTING GROUP INVESTIGATION

How to Implement

The implementation of a new teaching method requires that the school provide different forms of support and assistance to teachers. They must know that the principal and their colleagues consider the introduction of cooperative learning as part of the school's official policy and are willing to support it. Of great importance is the teachers' need not only for moral support from the school administration but for direct assistance in carrying out the new method in their classrooms. We have found that teacher self-help teams are an effective medium for providing the direct and constructive support that teachers need. These teams constitute a vital connecting link between the teachers' learning experiences in workshops and their actual practice of the Group Investigation method in the classroom.

The fundamental features of teacher self-help teams as we have employed them are: Three teachers plan a lesson together according to the principles of the Group Investigation method. One teacher implements the team's plan while the others observe the lesson. Afterwards they offer one another feedback about what occurred.

Teams of teachers will function effectively only after the teachers have worked together for some time, know one another, and can communicate with relative ease. It is advisable to have the teachers select their fellow team members themselves and to discuss their classroom work—their instructional preferences and style— before moving on to the next stages of this plan. Some experts on peer coaching in schools recommend that teachers experience an extended period of team building before they embark on the process outlined below. If the teachers in a particular school have had little or no exposure to collaborative work, a series of introductory sessions stressing communication skills and trust-building activities may be required (Graves & Graves, 1990; Joyce & Showers, 1987).

Our version of teacher self-help teams for implementing the Group Investigation method includes the following steps (S. Sharan & Hertz-Lazarowitz, 1978):

Figure 7.2   Teacher's Planning Sheet for Group Investigation

General Problem:

Stage 1.   Suggest possible subtopics.
How much time will be allotted for the Group Investigation project?
Teacher's role in this stage:

Stage 2.   Demonstrate how questions can be formulated for the study of each subtopic.
List a variety of resources for the students to use in carrying out their investigation.
Teacher's role in this stage:

Stage 3.   Describe one or two ways groups can carry out the investigation.
Discuss problems students might have at this stage and how you as teacher would assist them.
Teacher's role in this stage:

Stage 4.   Suggest ways students may prepare a final report.
Teacher's role in this stage:

Stage 5.   Suggest different ways students can present their final report.
Teacher's role in this stage:

Stage 6.   Suggest ways of assessing students' products as well as the process of working together as a group.
Teacher's role in this stage:

1. *Selecting team members.* It is not necessary for teams to include only teachers of the same grade level or subject matter. Often teachers from varied backgrounds prove more helpful to one another precisely because they see events differently and bring a range of experiences to the team. Most critical is the fact that the teachers should wish to work together. Generally a team has three

teachers. A larger number often creates problems of coordination. Having only two teachers per team results in an insufficient number of personnel for achieving the requisite level of objectivity.

2. *Planning a lesson.* Each team must specify the goals, content, and procedures to be implemented during a lesson according to the principles of the Group Investigation method. The plan must reflect the wishes of everyone involved. Most important, not only the content of the lesson but the details of group organization and management, consistent with the Group Investigation method, must be stated in operational terms, that is, what behavior by the teacher and students should be visible to observers during the lesson.

3. *Determining criteria for evaluation.* Team members should formulate a short list of three or four criteria for guiding the observers. The feedback to be offered after the lesson should be based on the criteria established in advance by the team.

4. *Observation.* One member of the team conducts a lesson while the other two teachers observe and record the behavior agreed upon earlier. It is often helpful to use an observation-recording sheet.

5. *Giving feedback.* As soon as the lesson ends, the team should meet and hear reports from the observers and from the teacher who conducted the lesson. After mentioning the positive features of the lesson observed, reports should focus on the problems encountered by the teacher who conducted the lesson as well as on the behavior recorded by the observers. The feedback session should include the planning of ways to deal with these problems.

6. *Repeat cycle.* The very same steps should be repeated so that each member of the team is observed and is able to observe each of his or her colleagues. Moreover, it is of great importance to repeat the entire cycle of planning and mutual observation more than once during a given academic year so that each teacher can demonstrate the implementation of a teaching plan that benefited from the feedback received from collegial evaluations.

What They Contribute

The outstanding feature of the method proposed here for teacher teams is the fact that decisions are made collectively by all the participants. The decisions made by the team relate to all major aspects of classroom instruction, such as the content of the lesson and the procedures to be followed in carrying out the plan of instruction. This makes possible a maximum degree of mutuality in the teachers' relationships. Such mutuality is critical if they are to accept one another's observations and criticisms of their teaching behavior as a basis for planning how to improve their implementation of the Group Investigation method during the next lesson.

Their experience in these teams demonstrates to teachers that they can learn more about their own teaching behavior from day to day and that there is no limit to one's potential growth as a teacher. This growth can be fostered by evaluation of one's classroom behavior by colleagues whose sole purpose is to contribute to their own professional skill and development. Evaluation through direct observation followed by constructive feedback focused on topics agreed upon in advance by all concerned is the key to this version of teacher teams for improving instruction. In our experience, teachers initially opposed to participating in these teams gradually learn to derive maximum benefit from them—and actually become dependent upon them for the support and collegial interest in their work that is otherwise lacking in many schools (S. Sharan et al., 1984; S. Sharan & Hertz-Lazarowitz, 1982).

The work of this kind of teacher team is directed as much at the *process* of teaching as it is at its content. That alone distinguishes this approach from the typical focus of educational evaluation. The team also conducts observations of the teachers' overt behavior that they themselves planned. This approach helps teachers concentrate on *how* to implement a Group Investigation session and does not focus exclusively on *what* the teacher is to say. The latter is the form of lesson plans most commonly stressed in schools.

Moreover, the observation of a particular teacher's classroom behavior is based upon instructional principles shared by all members of the team who have participated together in workshops on the Group Investigation method. This offers the teachers a set of shared goals and criteria by which to evaluate one another's work, rather than trying to derive a common set of guidelines from a very diverse collection of instructional preferences. While the latter will exist and affect the work of teacher teams in any case, the set of shared points of reference will make a team's task eminently more feasible and productive.

Some Impediments

Every form of human organization has problems that can make its operation difficult. Teacher teams are no exception. Personal and organizational problems can interfere with the functioning of these teams and even prevent the adoption by the school of new instructional methods. It is important to identify these problems and deal with them as effectively as possible.

The most common organizational problem confronting schools that wish to use teacher self-help teams is to arrange for two members of each team to have free time to observe their teammate conduct a lesson. This requires the principal to coordinate the schedules of the teachers involved in this project, or to provide substitute activities for these teachers' students while the teachers observe their colleagues' teaching.

We often hear teachers express many reservations about having colleagues present in the room during a lesson. These reservations, or even objections, are of different kinds, such as the following: Colleagues are not qualified to conduct objective observations of one's teaching behavior, nor would they necessarily know how to help in the improvement of one's teaching; the presence in the classroom of a colleague from the same school could expose the teacher to rumor and gossip; collegial evaluations could be misused and damage one's reputation in the school or become known to the principal or superintendent; colleagues could notice deficiencies in one's work that were not agreed upon in advance as the topics to be observed, and so forth.

The mutual observation of teaching behavior can present a threat to teachers. Most teachers are accustomed to teaching as a lone adult in the room "uninhibited" by the presence of other persons of equal professional status. Moreover, the assumption on which this entire approach is based conveys the message that the teaching behavior of the teachers involved can be improved and is not free of criticism. In order for the teams to fulfill their purpose, teachers must reach the point at which they can appreciate the potential benefits they will derive from participating in these teams. They must understand that these benefits far outweigh whatever fears they may have about the potential damage to them from having their work observed by their colleagues. It is advisable to bring up these potential difficulties and have teachers discuss them in advance of proceeding with the plan presented here.

Fear of criticism from colleagues will be radically reduced, even eliminated, if the school as a unit (i.e., the entire teaching staff) officially adopts this form of operation as a schoolwide norm. When teachers see that self-help teams are sanctioned, desired, and supported by the school administration and by their colleagues, they will be more inclined to accept this model of professional behavior without feeling threatened. Furthermore, if the teams are devoted to mutual assistance in the trial of new strategies, the innovations will be more likely to be sustained (Joyce & Showers, 1987).

Teachers will also develop positive attitudes toward their teams if team members are able to communicate well and offer constructive assistance to one another. Perhaps the principal can offer some in-service training to teachers on constructive patterns of interpersonal communication, if it becomes necessary. The success of a team in fulfilling its goals will determine whether teachers will wish to partici-pate. An atmosphere of cooperation among teachers created by the principal will make it possible for teacher self-help teams to operate effectively.

References

Adams, R. (1985). *Introductory biology in learning cycles.* Phoenix: Arizona Board of Regents.

Adcock, D., & Segal, M. (1983). *Play together, grow together.* New York: Mailman Family Press.

Archambault, R. (Ed.). (1964). *John Dewey on education: Selected writings.* Chicago: University of Chicago Press.

Arendt, H. (1958). *The human condition.* Chicago: University of Chicago Press.

Argyris, C. (1982). *Reasoning, learning and action.* San Francisco: Jossey-Bass.

Barbieri, E. (1988). Talents unlimited: One school's success story. *Educational Leadership, 45*(7), 35.

Barnes, D. (1969). *Language, the learner and the school.* Harmondsworth, England: Penguin.

Barnes, D. (1976). *From communication to curriculum.* Harmondsworth, England: Penguin.

Baron, J., & Sternberg, R. (Eds.). (1987). *Teaching thinking skills.* New York: Freeman.

Britton, J. (1976). *Language and learning.* London: Allan Lane.

Brubacher, M., & Payne, R. (1982). Team learning in the English classroom. *Indirections, 7*(4), 8–17.

Burns, M. (1987). *A collection of math lessons from grades 3 through 6.* New Rochelle, NY: Cuisenaire Company of America.

Cohen, E. (1984). The desegregated school: Problems in status, power and interethnic climate. In N. Miller & M. Brewer (Eds.), *Groups in contact* (pp. 77–96). Orlando, FL: Academic Press.

Cohen, E. (1986). *Designing groupwork: Strategies for the heterogeneous classroom.* New York: Teachers College Press.

Cohen, E., Lotan, R., & Catanzarite, L. (1990). Treating status problems in the cooperative classroom. In S. Sharan (Ed.), *Cooperative learning: Theory and research* (pp. 203–229). New York: Praeger.

DeCharms, R. (1968). *Personal causation.* New York: Academic Press.

Deci, E. (1975). *Intrinsic motivation.* New York: Plenum.

Dewey, J. (1943). *The school and society,* rev. ed. Chicago: University of Chicago Press.

Dias, P. (1979). Developing independent readers of poetry. *McGill's Journal of Education, 104*(2), 199–218.

Dias, P. (1985). Researching response to poetry—Part 1: A case for responding aloud protocols. *English Quarterly, 18*(4), 104–117.

Dias, P. (1990). I hate it when they agree: The collaborative re-creation of a poem. In M. Brubacher, R. Payne, & K. Rickett (Eds.), *Perspectives on small group learning: Theory and practice* (pp. 224–233). Oakville, Ontario: Rubicon.

Dishon, D., & O'Leary, P. (1984). *A guidebook for cooperative learning: A technique for creating more effective schools.* Holmes Beach, FL: Learning Publications.

Forrestal, P. (1990). Talking: Toward classroom action. In M. Brubacher, R. Payne, & K. Rickett (Eds.), *Perspectives on small group teaching: Theory and practice* (pp. 157–167). Oakville, Ontario: Rubicon.

Furth, H. (1969). *Piaget and knowledge.* Englewood Cliffs, NJ: Prentice-Hall.

Goodlad, J. (1984). *A place called school.* New York: McGraw-Hill.

Gorman, A. (1969). *Teachers and learners: The interactive process of education.* Boston: Allyn & Bacon.

Graves, N., & Graves, T. (1990). *What is cooperative learning? Tips for teachers and trainers* (2nd ed.). Santa Cruz: Cooperative College of California.

Harris, M., & Evans, M. (1972). *Case studies: Schools council environmental studies project.* London: Rupert Hart-Davis Edal.

Hassard, J. (1990). *Science experiences: Cooperative learning and the teaching of science.* Reading, MA: Addison-Wesley.

Hertz-Lazarowitz, R., & Davidson, J. (1990). *Six mirrors of the classroom: Pathway to a cooperative classroom.* Westlake Village, CA: Rajo Press.

Hertz-Lazarowitz, R., & Shachar, H. (1990). Teachers' verbal behavior in cooperative and whole-class instruction. In S. Sharan (Ed.), *Cooperative learning: Theory and research* (pp. 77–94). New York: Praeger.

Hertz-Lazarowitz, R., Sharan, S., & Steinberg, R. (1980). Classroom learning style and cooperative behavior of elementary school children. *Journal of Educational Psychology, 72,* 97–104.

Huhtala, J., & Coughlin, E. (1991). Group investigation, democracy and the Middle East: Team teaching English and government. *English Journal, 80*(5), 47–52.

Johnson, D., & Johnson, R. (1985). Motivational processes in cooperative, competitive and individualistic learning situations. In C. Ames & R. Ames (Eds.), *Research on motivation in education* (pp. 249–286). Orlando, FL: Academic Press.

Johnson, D., & Johnson, R. (1987). *Learning together and alone.* Englewood Cliffs, NJ: Prentice-Hall.

Johnson, D., & Johnson, R. (1988). *Creative conflict.* Edina, MN: Interaction Book Company.

Johnson, D., Johnson, R., & Holubec, E. (1986). *Circles of learning.* Edina, MN: Interaction Book Company.

Johnson, D., Johnson, R., & Maruyama, G. (1983). Interdependence and interpersonal attraction among heterogeneous individuals: A theoretical formulation and meta-analysis of the research. *Review of Educational Research, 53,* 5–54.

Johnson, D., Johnson, R., & Smith, K. (1986). Academic conflict among students: Controversy and learning. In R. Feldman (Ed.), *The social psychology of education* (pp. 199–231). Cambridge, England: Cambridge University Press.

Johnson, D., Maruyama, G., Johnson, R., Nelson, D., & Skon, L. (1981). Effects of cooperative, competitive and individualistic goal structures on achievement: A meta-analysis. *Psychological Bulletin, 89,* 47–62.

Joyce, B., & Showers, B. (1987). *Student achievement through staff development.* White Plains, NY: Longman.

Joyce, B., & Weil, M. (1986). *Models of teaching* (3rd ed.). Englewood Cliffs, NJ: Prentice-Hall.

Kagan, S. (1989). *Cooperative learning: Resources for teachers.* San Juan Capistrano, CA: Resources for Teachers.

Knapp, C., Swann, M., Vogl, S., & Vogl, R. (1986). *Using the outdoors to teach social studies: Grades 3–10.* Las Cruces, NM: ERIC/CRESS.

Kolb, D., & Fry, R. (1975). Towards an applied theory of experiential learning. In C. Cooper (Ed.), *Theories of group processes* (pp. 33–57). London: Wiley.

Kolb, D., & Lewis, L. (1986). Facilitating experiential learning: Observation and reflection. In L. Lewis (Ed.), *Experiential and simulation techniques for teaching adults.* San Francisco: Jossey-Bass.

Lazarowitz, R., & Karsenty, G. (1990). Cooperative learning and students' academic achievement, process skills, learning environment, and self esteem in tenth-grade biology classroom. In S. Sharan (Ed.), *Cooperative learning: Theory and research* (pp. 123–149). New York: Praeger.

Lewin, K. (1947a). Frontiers in group dynamics: Concept, method and reality in social science, social equilibria and social change. *Human Relations, 1,* 5–42.

Lewin, K. (1947b). Group decision and social change. In E. Maccoby, T. Newcomb, & E. Hartley (Eds.), *Readings in social psychology* (pp. 197–219). New York: Holt, Rinehart and Winston.

McCabe, M., & Rhoades, J. (1988). *The nurturing classroom.* Willits, CA: ITA Publications.

McClure, L., Cook, S., & Thompson, V. (1977). *Experience based learning: How to make the community your classroom.* Portland, OR: Northwest Regional Educational Laboratory.

Mctighe, J., & Lyman, F. (1988). Cueing thinking in the classroom: The promise of theory-embedded tools. *Educational Leadership, 45,* 18–24.

Miel, A. (1952). *Cooperative procedures in learning.* New York: Teachers College Press.

Miller, N., & Harrington, H. (1990). A situational identity perspective on cultural diversity and teamwork in the classroom. In S. Sharan (Ed.), *Cooperative learning: Theory and research* (pp. 39–75). New York: Praeger.

Moffett, J., & Wagner, B. A. (1983). *Student centered language arts and reading K–13: A handbook for teachers.* Boston: Houghton Mifflin.

Pea, R. (1982). What is planning development the development of? In D. Forbes & M. T. Greenberg (Eds.), *New directions for child development: Children's planning strategies* (pp. 5–27). San Francisco: Jossey-Bass.

Piaget, J. (1973). *To understand is to invent: The future of education.* New York: Grossman.

Robertson, L. (1990). Cooperative learning à la CLIP. In M. Brubacher, R. Payne, & K. Rickett (Eds.), *Perspectives on small group learning: Theory and practice* (pp. 185–201). Oakville, Ontario: Rubicon.

Ryan, R., Connell, J., & Deci, E. (1985). A motivational analysis of self-determination and self-regulation in education. In C. Ames & R. Ames (Eds.), *Research on motivation in education* (pp. 13–51). Orlando, FL: Academic Press.

Sarason, S. (1982). *The culture of the school and the problem of change* (2nd ed.). Boston: Allyn & Bacon.

Sarason, S. (1983). *Schooling in America: Scapegoat and salvation.* New York: Free Press.

Sarason, S. (1990a). *The challenge of art to psychology.* New Haven, CT: Yale University Press.

Sarason, S. (1990b). *The predictable failure of educational reform.* San Francisco: Jossey-Bass.

Sarason, S., Caroll, C., Maton, K., Cohen, S., & Lorentz, E. (1977). *Human services and resource networks.* San Francisco: Jossey-Bass.

Sarason, S., & Lorentz, E. (1979). *The challenge of the resource exchange network.* San Francisco: Jossey-Bass.

Schmuck, R., & Runkel, P. (1985). *The handbook of organization development in schools* (3rd ed.). Palo Alto, CA: Mayfield.

Schmuck, R., & Schmuck, P. (1988). *Group processes in the classroom* (5th ed.). Dubuque, IA: Brown.

Schön, D. (1987). *The reflective practitioner: How professionals think in action.* New York: Basic Books.

Sharan, S. (1980). Cooperative learning in small groups: Recent methods and effects on achievement, attitudes and ethnic relations. *Review of Educational Research, 50,* 241–271.

Sharan, S. (Ed.). (1990a). *Cooperative learning: Theory and research.* New York: Praeger.

Sharan, S. (1990b). Cooperative learning and helping behaviour in the multiethnic classroom. In H. Foot, M. Morgan, & R. Shute (Eds.), *Children helping children* (pp. 151–176). London: Wiley.

Sharan, S., Gal, I., & Stok, S. (1984). Tzavtei siyuah b'kerev segel hamorim bevait hasefer [Mutual assistance teams for teachers: A field experiment]. *Studies in Education* (Hebrew), *39*, 73–88.

Sharan, S., & Hertz-Lazarowitz, R. (1978). *Shituf peula vetikshoret bevait hasefer* [Cooperation and communication in schools]. Tel Aviv: Schocken.

Sharan, S., & Hertz-Lazarowitz, R. (1980). A group investigation method of cooperative learning in the classroom. In S. Sharan, P. Hare, C. Webb, & R. Hertz-Lazarowitz (Eds.), *Cooperation in education* (pp. 14–46). Provo, UT: Brigham Young University Press.

Sharan, S., & Hertz-Lazarowitz, R. (1982). Effects of an instructional change program on teachers' behavior, attitudes and perceptions. *Journal of Applied Behavioral Science, 18*, 185–201.

Sharan, S., Hertz-Lazarowitz, R., & Ackerman, Z. (1980). Academic achievement of elementary school children in small group versus whole class instruction. *Journal of Experimental Education, 48*, 125–129.

Sharan, S., Kussell, P., Hertz-Lazarowitz, R., Bejarano, Y., Raviv, S., & Sharan, Y. (1984). *Cooperative learning in the classroom: Research in desegregated schools.* Hillsdale, NJ: Erlbaum.

Sharan, S., & Rich, Y. (1984). Field experiments on ethnic integration in Israeli schools. In Y. Amir & S. Sharan (Eds.), *School desegregation* (pp. 189–217). Hillsdale, NJ: Erlbaum.

Sharan, S., & Shachar, H. (1988). *Language and learning in the cooperative classroom.* New York: Springer.

Sharan, S., & Shaulov, A. (1990). Cooperative learning, motivation to learn and academic achievement. In S. Sharan (Ed.), *Cooperative learning: Theory and research* (pp. 173–202). New York: Praeger.

Sharan, S., & Sharan, Y. (1976). *Small group teaching.* Englewood Cliffs, NJ: Educational Technology.

Sharan, Y., & Sharan, S. (1987). Training teachers for cooperative learning. *Educational Leadership, 45*, 20–25.

Sharan, Y., & Sharan, S. (1990). Group investigation expands cooperative learning. *Educational Leadership, 47*, 17–21.

Sigel, I., & Cocking, R. (1977). *Cognitive development from childhood to adolescence: A constructivist perspective.* New York: Holt, Rinehart and Winston.

Slavin, R. (1983a). *Cooperative learning.* White Plains, NY: Longman.

Slavin, R. (1983b). When does cooperative learning increase student motivation? *Psychological Bulletin, 94*, 429–445.

Slavin, R. (1986). *Educational psychology: Theory into practice.* Englewood Cliffs, NJ: Prentice-Hall.

Slavin, R. (1987). Developmental and motivational perspectives on cooperative learning: A reconciliation. *Child Development, 58*, 1161–1167.

Slavin, R. (1990). *Cooperative learning: Theory, research and practice*. Englewood Cliffs, NJ: Prentice-Hall.

Stanford, G., & Stanford, B. D. (1969). *Learning discussion skills through games*. New York: Citation Press.

Stivers, E., & Wheelan, S. (Eds.). (1986). *The Lewin legacy: Field theory in current practice*. Berlin, Germany: Springer-Verlag.

Thelen, H. (1954). *Dynamics of groups at work*. Chicago: University of Chicago Press.

Thelen, H. (1960). *Education and the human quest*. New York: Harper.

Thelen, H. (1967). Group interactional factors in learning. In E. Bower & W. Hollister (Eds.), *Behavioral science frontiers in education* (pp. 257–287). New York: Wiley.

Thelen, H. (1981). *The classroom society*. London: Croom Helm.

Weitz, J., & Cameron, A. (1985). Individual differences in the student's sense of control. In C. Ames & R. Ames (Eds.), *Research on motivation in education* (pp. 93–140). Orlando, FL: Academic Press.

Wells, G., Chang, G., & Maher, A. (1990). Creating classroom communities of literate thinkers. In S. Sharan (Ed.), *Cooperative learning: Theory and research* (pp. 95–121). New York: Praeger.

Wiederhold, C. (1990). *Cooperative learning and critical thinking: The question matrix*. San Juan Capistrano, CA: Resources for Teachers.

Yaakobi, D., & Sharan, S. (1985). Teacher beliefs and practices: The discipline carries the message. *Journal of Education for Teaching, 11*, 187–199.

Index

About the Authors

Yael Sharan is coordinator of in-service teacher training for the Israel Educational Television Center. She also conducts workshops for trainers and for principals on cooperative learning for the ministry of education, and serves on a national committee that is preparing a cooperative learning handbook for teacher training colleges in Israel.

Shlomo Sharan is professor of educational psychology at the School of Education, Tel-Aviv University, Tel-Aviv, Israel, where he has been teaching since 1966. Along with colleagues, he was instrumental in founding (1979) the International Association for the Study of Cooperation in Education and served as its president from 1982 to 1988. He is the author of many books and articles on cooperative learning and on school organization and development. Yael and Shlomo Sharan are co-authors of two earlier books, *The Psychology and Remediation of Learning Disabilities*, in Hebrew (1969) and *Small Group Teaching*, published in Hebrew (1974), English (1976), and German (1976). Shlomo Sharan is editor of *Cooperative Learning: Theory and Research* (1990).